MY SON THE JOCK

by GERALD GREEN

Nonfiction

My Son the Jock
The Stones of Zion
The Artists of Terezin
The Portofino PTA
His Majesty O'Keefe
    (with Lawrence Klingman)

Fiction

Tourist
Blockbuster
Faking It
To Brooklyn with Love
The Legion of Noble Christians
The Heartless Light
The Lotus Eaters
The Last Angry Man
The Sword and the Sun

MY SON
THE JOCK

Gerald Green

PRAEGER PUBLISHERS
New York

Published in the United States of America in 1975
by Praeger Publishers, Inc.
111 Fourth Avenue, New York, N.Y. 10003

Library of Congress Cataloging in Publication Data
Green, Gerald.
    My son the jock.
    1. Green, David, 1956– I. Title
PS3513.R4447Z65   813'.5'4 [B]   74-15677
ISBN 0-275-19820-0

Printed in the United States of America

For
Coach Stanley
and
the King School Football Team, 1973

Know ye not that they which run in a race run all, but that one re-ceiveth the prize? So run that ye may obtain. — *Corinthians* 1:24

(Sign in the office of Buzz Stanley, football coach at King School)

I cannot understand how a human bean cannot know how to block.
—Lou Little

1

Before the colors fade I must get this down.

Early November in Connecticut: bright sky, a sniff of frost in the air. The football turf and the oaks and beeches that circle it are still green. On the field, two prep school teams are in the closing minutes of a tense game.

Football has always seemed to me a carefully organized disaster. I've never played it, but I've watched more of it than is good for my vision and nervous system, and while it diverts and excites me, it also fills me with a vague fear. Chaotic, violent, yet planned down to minuscule details, it is a game that inevitably means tragedy and humiliation for one side and exuberant gloating for the other. More tears are shed in football locker rooms, I suspect, than backstage at beauty contests. Losing at football generates a terror and a shame that seem to be absent from other games. All that brutal rehearsing and drill, physical hurt and abuse, memorizing of formations and plays as complex as the notations of a theoretical physicist. When you lose, you lose all.

Now I'm stumbling along the sidelines of the King School field. With me are two other middle-aged men, Norm Fieber and Murray Levison. Like me, they have sons playing for King. It's homecoming day. The three of us comprise about one-tenth of the rooters on the King side. We're hoarse. Our faces are splotched with crimson. I wonder if our sons resent our vicarious aggressiveness?

After all, it's their game. They're the ones taking the lumps, getting bruised and drubbed. Who are we to scream so much?

"The kids *can't* blow this one," Murray Levison says. "They just can't. This is one they've got to win."

"They'll win, they'll win," Norm Fieber says.

I say nothing, because in my secret heart I have already told myself that King will lose again. There is a minute and a half left to play. King School is leading St. Hugh's 8-0. Thus far the record is five losses and one tie. King has come close in several games. My son David, co-captain, linebacker, nose guard, pulling guard, assures me the record should be three and three. But he knows as well as I do that *should be* is never the same as *is*. If they fail today against St. Hugh's they will be remembered (thanks to our hometown daily, *The Stamford Advocate*) as "winless" King. The *Advocate* has already christened them "hapless" King, the team that lost a 62-6 "laugher" to mighty St. Luke's. Gentlemen sportswriters, those are *our* sons you are talking about. Typical media irresponsibility—except for the fact that it's the truth.

A time-out. David trots to the sidelines with the King quarterback, Jimmy Wilson, to talk with Coach Buzz Stanley. My son's face is muddy, sweaty, feverish. His eyes are an angry dark brown under the white helmet. (King's colors are maroon and white. The uniforms are white trimmed with maroon, and the team wears maroon helmets, except for the captain, who rates a *white* helmet. I learn after the season that it is a special "Redell" water helmet, because David likes to block and tackle with his head. This information is never relayed to my wife.)

"You guys stink," I hear Coach Buzz Stanley saying to his "men," who range in age from fourteen to seventeen. "You blow this one I'm finished with you."

They call David "Mean Joe" after the towering defensive tackle on the Pittsburgh Steelers. He's a bit smaller at 5' 9" and 175 pounds, but he hits hard, or, as I have learned to say, he *sticks*. At the moment I wish he were a pale Talmudic scholar, soft-handed, bearded, a boy with 1400 College Boards and a cool intellectual future. The fantasy vanishes. I wallow in his physicality. He's a way I never was, never will be.

"Suck up your guts, get out there and start hitting," Coach Stanley says. David nods, looks at Jimmy Wilson, trots back onto the field. His willingness—eagerness—to obey Stanley's command astonishes me. David, our second son, youngest of three, has never taken kindly to authority. He has resisted parents, teachers, counselors, policemen. He isn't a bad kid, just a fiercely independent one. But Coach Robert B. Stanley III, "the Buzzer," can insult him, shove him, order him about, drag him through the dirt—and he loves it. At least he seems to love it.

King must win today or it will be a long gray winter. It has been a season of fumbles, penalties, bad breaks, games stolen by "homers"—referees favoring the home team—and lost by King's own inexperience and lack of confidence. I reassure myself that David and his friends will get over their disappointment at this season of small cheer. But what about the fathers? What about Levison and Fieber and Jack Rutledge and Warren Eginton and all the other aging athletes-manqués who have suffered with the boys? I cannot speak for the others, but I know I will awaken at three in the morning ten years from now and agonize over this so-far winless season.

King's ball. It's almost over. All they have to do is control the game, hang on to that 8-0 lead. David is the right guard, next to his co-captain, center Paul LeBlanc. On the other side is Andy Levison, a tackle. Jimmy Wilson poises over LeBlanc's raised behind. In back of Wilson are the running backs, big Bobby Fieber and a spindly, wide-eyed boy named Cameron Sillars. Sam Boe is the flanker.

A mad impulse races through my fevered brain: I'll win the game for David. Race out on the field and do something heroic. I'll bribe the referee. Dope St. Hugh's Gatorade. It's useless. These are psychotic manifestations of my own meager physical attainments, my lackadaisical attitude toward winning. Small comforts surface in my brain—if they lose, at least he played the game.

And never, never did he quit or show fear or give less than his best. These are things that could never be said of his paunchy, short-winded, weak-ankled, nearsighted father.

"Who in hell is running that clock?" Norm Fieber asks. "It hasn't moved."

Yes, I see it. A plot. They'll keep the clock running so that St. Hugh's can win in the fading minutes.

"Stick 'em, Andy," Levison shouts to his son.

"Go get 'em, Dave," I add. A widening chasm is forming in my duodenum.

The bodies swarm and churn as Fieber hits the line. No gain. *Move, clock! End, game!* We all fear that if they don't beat St. Hugh's they will end the season without a victory. Next week is the last game—with Hackley, a team of monsters.

The scene blurs before my eyes. The cheerleaders, nymphets from King's sister-school, Low-Heywood, prance and pirouette in front of us. Saddle shoes, white knee socks, maroon panties, maroon skirts, white sweaters. Everything tilts: the barn-red buildings, the white-lined turf, the rickety grandstand, the thwacking bodies on the field.

Again, no gain. What's happened to the King ground game? They will have to give up the ball. The crack and splat of leather, young bodies, foam padding shiver me. "Can you enjoy this?" I have asked David after a brutal practice session, when he comes home taped, bruised, smelling of liniment. "Sure I do," he growls. "You think I'd do it if I didn't? I like to stick guys." (And his father ran from street fights at his age.)

Rutledge, Eginton, other nervous fathers join us. Roy Boe, owner of the New York Nets and the New York Islanders, walks by. We take heart from his unflappability, his professional cool. A man who bankrolls Julius Erving will not suffer his son, King's flanker back, to lose all his games.

But will that clock never move?

A sweep. Bobby Fieber is carrying the ball, dragging tacklers. David leads the blocking. He slams his 175 pounds into the St.

Hugh's linebacker, a lumbering boy with a paunch. David hurls helmet, chest, arms at him. The move is timed perfectly. The linebacker crumbles, atomized. Yes! More! *Stick!*

Fieber spins the wrong way, into another player's arms. No first down. Buzz will complain all year about Bobby, All-League, powerful, fearless. "The kid is great," Coach Stanley tells me, "but he's got this thing about spinning toward the sidelines. If I could put the sidelines in the end zone he'd score ten times every game."

Stanley, old riverboat gambler, calls for a pass. We can't believe it. The game's almost over, and he's passing? Matt Gormley, a second-string back with a first-rate arm, 120 pounds, takes a snap from the center (another Buzzian trick) and lets fly. It's batted down. The clock stops. Portents of doom. I can write the ending. We punt. They score.

Fieber punts from King's twenty-seven-yard line. There's crisp downfield coverage. David leads the charge that brings down the St. Hugh's returner. Clock stops again. And so we stand and wait, frozen and fearful on a darkening November day, and we try to stifle the inevitable bronze taste of defeat. King will lose again. We will suffer through one more Saturday night of watching the grieving faces of our sons, knowing their unshed tears, feeling the pain of their fractures, concussions, sprains, shin-splints, and, worst of all, their recriminations. Who missed a block? Who dropped a pass? Who was offside?

Andy Levison, Cam Sillars, and Dave blast the St. Hugh's quarterback. (I must explain that almost the entire King team plays both offense and defense; only thirteen or fourteen players of the squad of twenty-two ever get into a game.) There's a whiff of victory in the air, as pungent as a good red Bordeaux opened on a patio on a summer's day. The enemy quarterback has trouble rising. ("They were grunting," Dave says later. "They felt it when we stuck.")

A desperation pass by St. Hugh's. They flood the field with blue and gold receivers. Sillars intercepts. I'm glad it's Cam. He is a tenth-grader, wide-eyed, shy, teased a great deal, forever astonished.

"Thirty seconds left," Norm Fieber says. "This is it. They run the clock out and we win."

"Right," Murray Levison adds. "They might even beat Hackley next week. They looked good today."

The nymphets shriek: "Stick 'em, King."

Ah, their tender knees and toothsome thighs. Suddenly I am Humbert Humbert, craving their innocent flesh.

"Stick 'em, Green," a cheerleader shouts. She confides to a sister temptress. "Dave's our best defensive player. He'll stick 'em."

No girl ever said that of me. Like certain hillbillies I knew in the army, I should have tattooed on my right forearm "Born to Lose." Is it all my fault? Is defeat contagious? Have I infected my seventeen-year-old son and the whole team?

"It's over," Fieber insists. "Two more plays."

Norm is an optimist. It's never over. Jimmy Wilson keeps, races in his loping gait for the sidelines. Hemmed in, he tries to lateral to Bobby Fieber, is hit, fumbles. The ball vanishes under a mob of blue and gold jerseys.

Sixteen seconds left. I want to berate Norm for putting the whammy on us. Nothing ever ends. Not for those marked by fate to double-fault, fumble, drop pop flies.

The fathers gather behind the King bench. Coach Stanley is raging. "I warn you guys," Buzz says, "you blow this, you'll scrimmage for an hour when the whistle blows. I'll run your asses ragged. The season is riding on this. Stop them."

It's unfair. I look at the team—Green, LeBlanc, Levison, Eginton, Rutledge, Wilson, Sillars. They have suffered so much, gained so little. Why lose when you don't even have to compete? Last year King failed to field a varsity football team for the first time in its history. Not enough players. This season, thanks to Dave and the other diehards, they coaxed enough boys to play. But four of the school's best athletes disdained the game. They knew it would be a losing season. Where are they now, those no-shows?

The snap again. We all know what St. Hugh's will do. They have a giant playing end. I don't know his name. He is 6′ 4″ and weighs 240 pounds. He is much too big. Buzz moves David to an outside linebacker position to take on the monster. By now my son knows the giant well. He has been blocking him on running plays all afternoon, chased him half the length of the field earlier.

The quarterback is pursued. Hands clutch at him. Everyone is exhausted. David tries to play bump and run on a man weighing 65 pounds more than he does. He manages to slow the end, bounces off him, staggers. Screams reverberate in my skull. Why doesn't everyone go home?

A dreadful ending writes itself in my brain. A long pass. The giant rises above them, reaches high over Dave's 5′ 9″, gathers in the ball, galumphs into the end zone. Touchdown. A two-point conversion. King is tied 8-8 by a team it destroyed all afternoon, a team of grunters who did not like to stick, or get stuck. It will be a long, sad winter in the Green home.

Why in God's name have I encouraged my son in this violent lunacy? And why does he insist on torturing himself in this contest of pain and humiliation, this ballet of broken bones, torn ligaments and shredded pride?

David started playing football at King in the sixth grade. He was eleven years old, short, chunky, neckless, dark, ill-tempered. I have a color photograph of him in uniform before a game with Greenwich Academy. The shoulder pads make him wider than he is tall. His pants end an inch above his cleats. He scowls at my Pentax with uncompromising brown eyes. In this child, our youngest, the dark blood of his mother's Neapolitan ancestors, spiced with Arab and Greek strains, predominates. There is no sign of the prayerful, cerebral, apologetic, introspective Semite—my contribution. This lack may explain those headlong blocks and crunching tackles.

I remember the first time I saw the King sixth-grade team play. They won, beating Brunswick. King's star was the quarterback, a tiny black boy named Peter Fisher. Pete wasn't much over four feet tall and may have weighed 85 pounds. But he ran like an eleven-year-old Jesse Owens. King's big scoring play was the quarterback sneak. David and the center would open a hole. Pete would squirt through and run as far as he could, as fast as he could. A play designed for short yardage, it often resulted in scoring dashes of forty, fifty, even sixty yards.

It was remarkable that the sixth grade could field a team at all. King is a small school. The last senior class graduated twenty-nine boys. Yet somehow, enough eleven-year-olds were found, an eager if poorly assorted and oddly shaped group. They came in all sizes and conformations—beanpole thin, roly-poly, minuscule like Fisher, hugely fat.

They were coached by Mr. Burns, a gentle, scholarly man with a Ford Madox Ford mustache, who taught mathematics. During time-outs, Mr. Burns would diagram plays in the dirt, using a broken stick. The games were played on murky afternoons in country fields. Or is my memory dramatizing these events, coating them with a brown-beige hue? It's all become misty, the figures moving slowly, the cries of players and spectators sounding like echoes. I went through those early seasons in a haze of incredulity. I could not believe that I, the four-eyed sissy of Prospect Place, could have a son who played football.

King 21, Brunswick 0. Three touchdowns by Pete Fisher, racing past young WASPs, black, tiny, uncatchable. The King sixth-graders would run out double file before the game, giving throat to a roaring hum, taught by the gentle Burns. Where had I heard that throaty rumble before? I remembered: in the film *War and Peace*—the Russian version—when the Imperial officers salute General Kutuzov. An undulant, wolflike wail. What did Burns have in mind? These were tots who got tangled in their jock-straps and wept hot tears when they lost.

My own tired eyes were also moist the first time I saw the King team clap hands, break from the huddle, and get into position for the first offensive play. *Set. Down. Blue, thirty-two on six. Hut, hut.* Forever Peter Fisher runs through my head.

"How was David's game?" Marie asked me. "Did he play?"

"Sure. He starts. He played guard, center, linebacker. You can't miss him."

"Oh?"

"He's the shortest player, the second fattest, and except for two black kids, Peter Fisher and Gary Macauley, he's the darkest."

"Did he get hurt?"

"No. Dave can handle himself. And they beat the socks off Brunswick."

Already the virus of surrogate violence was in my thin blood. Like Jarring Jack Jackson, Eddie Mayhoff's alumnus boob in the Jerry Lewis film *That's My Boy*, I was for better or worse inextricably involved with my son's athletic career. I would be miserable with him, feel his pain, guilt, anger, joy.

Athletic genes are sparse in the Green family. There is no evidence in our genealogical tables of people who like to stick. Marie, myself, our two older children tend to be bookish, ruminative types. Nancy, our daughter, is intense, articulate, into Transcendental Meditation after the pressure cooker of Brandeis University. Ted, our elder son, is bearded, thin, quiet, on the board of the *Columbia Daily Spectator*. Neither of these two offspring nor their parents have good backhands. We are all more at home in libraries than at net. And then came David Nicholas Green, neckless and strong. We cannot fathom him. He is the mutant in our midst.

Six years after he began to play football, now that he was captain of his school team, I found myself still pleading with my wife to come and see him play.

"I hate football," Marie says. "It's stupid and vicious. Why must he play at all?"

"It's his life."

"No, it's *yours*. Let him learn something he can use, like tennis or golf. Better, let him study more and get his grades up."

She'll never understand. What do good grades mean to me, who made Phi Beta Kappa at Columbia but hardly ever won a fist fight in Brooklyn? But she is an Italo-American. She has prior rights to toughness. Her Americanism can never be in doubt. In her lineage are welterweights, policemen, and one mysterious *goombah,* now deceased, who ran things for Meyer Lansky in Havana. Nothing need be proved. Descended from hard guys and dropouts, she proudly graduated magna cum laude at age thirty-six (having gone to work at eighteen, like all good Italian girls in the Bronx), went on to an M.A. and a successful career teaching learning-disabled children. She doesn't need football.

"Be tolerant," I say to Marie. "Let's say both David and I need his football. I stand before you paunchy, bald, fearful, afflicted with a daily migraine, contemplating a lost youth and the courage I never had when I needed it."

"I know. You never won a fight."

"Well, once."

Some autobiographical data are needed at this point in order to understand why, at fifty-two with fourteen published books and scores of television documentaries to my credit, I stop strangers and bray: "My son made the All-Fairchester League football team." Or the time I was on a radio talk show and, in the midst of a discussion of Watergate, blurted out: "I have a son who plays middle linebacker, middle guard, and pulling guard." This was followed by five seconds of dead air and a suspicion in the host's mind that he had once again been saddled with a nut guest.

Let's get it out. These enthusiasms grow out of a boyhood cursed with weak ankles, slowness, poor eyesight from too many hours of reading, flabby muscles, straight A's in school, and a saintly, intellectual mother who taught me to run from fights ("Reason with them"), never to provoke anyone, and cross the street if I saw any mean boys approaching.

Such counsel served me ill in Brownsville, a crumbling Brooklyn neighborhood that prided itself on its gangsters and pugilists. We had our choice in those days. We could admire monsters like Abe (Kid Twist) Reles, Blue-Jaw Magoon, and Frank (The Dasher) Abbadando, all of whom came to bad ends, or choose as heroes the two-fisted, crowd-pleasing lightweights and welterweights who fought at the Eastern Parkway Arena and the Ridgewood Grove. Schoolboy Bernie Friedkin. Yussel Goldstein. Solly Krieger. Even if you didn't box, you grew up admiring these rugged coreligionists who proved, before the Israeli Army won its victories, that Jews could fight.

We were good boys who did not cut class, were bar-mitzvah'd, and went to college or started small businesses. But we knew all about the hard punchers and fancy dans, learned the importance of toughness, courage, the firm jaw, the narrowed eyes, the line drawn in the dirt. One never backed down. One accepted challenges. One took one's lumps. So went the street wisdom. I knew all this, but it didn't seem to help. Oversized but soft and slow, my brain reeling under my mother's admonitions to be wary of bad boys, I won only one fight in my life, against Sambo Schwartz. Dimly, I recall I once fought a draw with Bobby Gobelman. Both boys were a head shorter than I was, but strong and shifty.

A win and a draw. On both occasions I had been tormented beyond endurance. *Sister Mary. Four-eyes. Scared to go in da gutter.* Incredibly, at age eleven I was forbidden by my mother to go into the gutter, to dare to step off the sidewalk, to violate the iron boundary of the curb. I lived in mortal terror of her catching her criminally inclined son straying into the path of a speeding Hupmobile. This in 1933, when automobiles were as scarce as good jobs.

Sambo Schwartz was my age, smaller, a "terrific athlete." As I look back over my Brownsville youth, it seems that all the boys I knew were "terrific athletes." Or was it that I always tagged after the good punchball and handball players? Somewhere there must have been poorly coordinated boys like myself, squinting into Ralph Henry Barbour novels.

A spring night in the malformed schoolyard of Public School 144. For no reason other than his temporary boredom with handball, Sambo dances around me. "Sister Mary, Sister Mary," he croons. "Ascared to go in da gutter. Four-eyes, four-eyes." He has freckles and brown hair. Not a bad kid by any means. It was simply part of the nocturnal ritual on Prospect Place. The doctor's son with the sissy name, Gerald. A failure at punchball.

Rage exploded in my chest. I had taken all the abuse I intended to take. Never again. The draw with Bobby Gobelman, I now recall, was fought a few months earlier under identical provocation. Lunging at Sambo, I flailed my arms, connecting with solid *clacks* on his freckled cheeks and forehead. What demon possessed me? My fists were almost apologetic as they cracked against his astonished face. The fight lasted seconds. He retreated and wept. Jos Dratel and Stanley Budesa, elder statesmen of the gang, pulled me off. They made us shake hands. I was magnanimous in victory. All agreed that I was in the right, that I had been tormented beyond forbearance.

There was no sweetness in that victory. I went home, sat in the kitchen, and cried. My father, that irascible, muscular, frustrated tower of outrage, found me swallowing huge chunks of misery while trying to drink a quart of cold milk. His love for me was boundless and embarrassing, but he could never understand a son who ran from fights.

"What happened?" he shouted. "Who picked on you? I'll knock their blocks off. Lice! Scum of the earth! Picking on a child!"

"Nobody picked on me," I wailed. "I won a fight."

"Who with? I'll tear the galoots apart."

"I said I won. I wo-o-o-n."

"Then what are you bawling about like a mollycoddle?" He stalked off in search of my mother. "Anna? Where are you? You see what you did to him? You made him a milksop. He wins a fight and he cries about it."

What the devil *was* I sobbing about? I'd won, hadn't I? I'd beat up my tormentor. Was I sorry for Sambo? Possibly. Or perhaps I was sorry for all of us—in dubious battle, living out our lives in crumbling schoolyards playing box ball and kickety-can.

My father decided once again that I needed "boxing lessons." From age five, when I had staggered into the house with my first bloody nose, this fantasy of boxing lessons would arise. Elaborate plans were formulated. My father had been a gym teacher at Savage Institute before going to medical school. Now he swore he would look up an old colleague, preferably some tough Irishman, and *he* would train me in the subtleties of the left jab and the right cross. Or perhaps his friend Dr. Harry Koster, the legendary surgeon and a gentleman boxer and wrestler, might be induced to work with me. Nothing like this ever happened. I was more terrified of lessons than of Bobby Gobelman.

Each man must confront himself from time to time and ask— who am I? What am I? Where have I failed? Even such lords of the earth as Nelson Rockefeller, Richard Burton, Normal Mailer, and Muhammad Ali must awaken at three in the morning, rub their itchy scalps, stare in the bathroom mirror, and in the cruel fluorescent light ask themselves painful questions. As the set points elude me more frequently, I have come to accept the terrible truth of Coach Buzz Stanley's verdict on mankind. "The world is made up of two kinds of people," the Buzzer says. "Those who stick and those who don't. Your son Dave sticks." And he tells me of big, strong players for King or on their opponents' teams. "But they don't stick. Dave sticks."

There it is. There is the measure of my failure, of the gap between us. I know it now. I never stuck, never had a chance to, would have been afraid to stick. Beating up Sambo Schwartz, I wept for him, for myself, for everyone.

Neurotic ramblings apart, I have never been keen on pain. Migraine has afflicted me since I was sixteen. For years I suffered weekly bouts of intractable, disabling pain. Hours have I sat in dark rooms, full of agony, icepack pressed to my temples, my arteries constricted with ergotomine, praying for the throbbing to end. And I have had kidney stones, fractures, high fevers. I have enjoyed none of them. Nor did I emerge from these experiences a "better man."

But . . . to go out of one's way to accept pain and inflict it? Perhaps we should admit that part of our fascination with football is its very violence, the way in which strong men are brought to earth, suffering torn ligaments, shredded cartileges, broken bones. No, I tell myself. That's only a small part. Football is scientific, suspenseful, the supreme team effort. It is timing, execution, grace, strength, speed. The pain is incidental. (Then why do all the recent books "exposing" football—fiction and nonfiction—stress the players' consumption of codeine, Demerol, uppers, downers? Are all the writers vengeful cranks? Or are they telling us a horrible truth?)

Yet I must believe that it is more than a battle of sly, mean, pain-inflicting brutes. Glancing through Coach Stanley's playbook, I am astonished that teenage boys—most of them indifferent scholars—can absorb so much. The game seems no less complex than algebra or physics. And as for such accepted nonsense courses as "The Art of Sci-Fi Film" or "Ethics, Humor, and Minorities," they are simply not in the same intellectual class with the four-three zone defense and the five-three stack.

Football players should surely receive academic credit for their labors. Why not? College juniors get credit for papers on "Symbolism in the Films of Sam Peckinpah" and "Early Television and the Stand-up Comic." Memorizing and acting out the counter series off-tackle is considerably more difficult. You must learn it the way you learn the binomial theorem, and you must do it well or you will be physically drubbed and, worse, may lose the game.

But in criticism—film for the most part, but this applies as well to art, literature, dance—anything can be said, any position defended, any nonsense presented as the Koran. Fearlessly, the critic may be wrong-headed, arbitrary, self-contradictory. So long as he writes reasonably well (and that qualification also seems to be going by the board) he can get away with anything. But the repercussions of a missed block or a dropped handoff are swift and sure. The hapless player is not given the privilege of discussing with the coach the subtle nuances that caused him to be boxed in or blocked out, to miss a tackle.

Maybe I protest too much about football's precision, its intellectual side, its heroic qualities. I confess that I remain ambivalent. Through the long fall and winter season I am glued to the TV set. Eyes glazed, jaw slack, brain numb, I watch the interminable games. After an hour, the *chock* and *thock* of armored giants becomes boring. I barely hear the *hut-hut*. But I watch anyway, wondering sometimes with a counter-culturist's sneaky joy whether the game is doomed. The pro game, at least, seems to have become repetitious. Off tackle, sweep, pass. The determining factor always appears to be, can Team A's receivers beat Team B's pass defenders? One keeps hearing the announcers pick out a tight end or a wide receiver as the "key man." Obviously the men defending against his receptions are equally key. So we watch the patterns emerge as these lean, fast men from Grambling and Alcorn A & M play out their personal feuds. It can be exciting. It can also be boring and predictable. In *Semi-Tough*, Dan Jenkins says it with vulgar candor. His white hero is asked if his team will win the Super Bowl. "Yeah," he drawls, "our niggers is better than their niggers." (It's true. Where would we be without black athletes? They simply happen to be better at catching passes and knocking them down. It isn't their fault that Whitey has maneuvered them into what may be a vanishing sport.)

And still we watch, corneas trembling, retinas shivering. *Jurgensen really got leveled. Simpson's hurt, he's favoring his ankle. What a block—he never knew what hit him.* It is a bone-breaking, muscle-bruising game played by huge, strong, fast, merciless men. Yet how we all yearn to be part of it! We long to wear our jockstraps outside our trousers, to carry the ball on third and three, twisting past the first-down markers, to trade clever quips with Alex Karras and Howard and the Giffer, to seek our Badge of Courage. Yet there are moments when I never want to see another game or read another sports page. In my coward's way, I applaud the injuries, torn ligaments, broken ribs. Serves those unfeeling clods right. Why should they dominate the public mind, capture our eyes and ears and hearts?

Flee, churlish thoughts! Those who play the game are braver than I ever was. They lay it on the line. They stick. Athletes who endure pain have always intrigued me. Those who manifest sheer courage, grace under pressure, are even more fascinating. The first heroes of my youth were the aforementioned Jos Dratel and Stanley Budesa, the greatest punchball players in the history of Brownsville, at least *ca.* 1931–37. Jos played "center" for the Prospect Place Pirates. Stanley was the lone "outfielder." They were as magnificent in the mastery of their skills—punchball was a blindingly fast game—as were the baseball gods of my youth, Mungo, Stripp, Lopez.

Budesa once ran half a city block to catch the only three-sewer hit ever seen on Prospect Place. Dratel was a wonder at center, a kind of middle-of-the-street shortstop, sliding, leaping, skinning his knees, elbows, and arms in miraculous catches of the spinning rubber Spaulding. But beyond that, they were *fearless*. Punchball was not a violent game. But the contests between neighborhood teams often degenerated into bloody fights.

As official scorekeeper, I stood on the sidelines with my dog-eared notebook of box scores and statistics and watched the whirling fists and pummeling arms with hideous delight. The sound of hard knuckles landing on bone is loud and clear in my ears even today. Forty years ago I saw Jos Dratel, a fair-skinned, curly-headed boy of fourteen, battle it out with a ruffian two years older and six inches taller, captain of a rival team, who was reputed to have been a Golden Gloves novice. He was also the "kid brudda" of a Murder, Inc., hit man. Jos was not impressed. He sought no help, made no excuses, backed down not an inch when the ogre sprang at him, fangs bared, mouth hurling curses we never used. They flailed at each other's skulls, cheeks, throats, arms, drawing blood, raising welts, until men pulled them apart. The bully, a banana-nosed troglodyte who had once spit in my eye and kneed me in the crotch because he imagined I had mocked him—I was innocent, Lord, how innocent I was!—appeared more eager than Jos to quit.

Budesa, slender, bespectacled, tow-headed, was the only Pole on a team of Jewish boys. Like Lord Jim, he was "one of us." He was polite and well-spoken. In his teens he took to reading Emily Post so that he might improve his conversation with young ladies. Like Dratel, he was a born leader.

A memory: the schoolyard of PS 144, the same colosseum where I won my fight with Sambo Schwartz. We are playing softball in early spring. The softball is mine—new, ivory white, smelling richly of blanched leather. It is stitched with those curious high ridges of the old "indoor baseball." (Do they make them that way any more?) Normally I am chosen last, after the Schwartzes and Gobelmans, and some days I am Odd Man Out and do not get to play at all. But this bright Sunday morning I am much desired: I have brought the new ball. Budesa, my captain, assigns me to the outfield, which means I must play on the street side of a high iron fence, segregated from the rest.

I don't mind. It's warm, clear, and I'm playing. As a matter of fact the only skill I ever learned well in baseball was catching flies. I pound my mitt and wait. In seconds, I am frightened. Black enemies lurk on St. Mark's Place. Ragged, heedless, contemptuous of our prettily organized game, they lie in wait in doorways, behind ashcans. I notice a classmate—Lee Roy Bishop. "Hi, Lee Roy," I say. My tremulous voice is full of fake amiability.

"You sheet," Lee Roy says. Even in 1934 they knew me for what I was: Goldberg, the two-faced liberal.

"You chicken," another boy says.

They are both proved right a few minutes later. Big Willie Adleman blasts my softball over the fence, over my head. It rolls across St. Mark's Place. Lee Roy scoops it up. He and his friends run away. End of softball. End of game.

I stand in my tracks, frozen with terror and despair. No one moves inside the playground. The unwritten law among us is: Let them alone, don't start with them. Even if you win a fight, they come back with their fathers and uncles. The thieves vanish down Howard Avenue.

Suddenly Stanley Budesa is vaulting the iron fence and, in tattered sneakers, is running after them like the wind across the Polish plain. His unhooked gray knickers flap in the breeze. Inspired by his reckless courage, Jos, Big Willie, and the rest of our gang leap over the fence. I bring up the rear.

Halfway down Howard Avenue, Stanley plunges into the heart of the mob, bowls Lee Roy over, wrestles with him, and, ignoring the blows and kicks of the dark avengers, retrieves the ball. They see Jos and Big Willie, curse us, spit at Stanley, and race away, mocking us with wild cries. But we have the ball back; the game will go on.

To this day I marvel at Budesa's act. Why did he ignore the odds, the possibility of a hidden knife or bicycle chain? He was not very big and not renowned as a fighter. Stanley was graceful and swift, but he was not a "tough" boy. Before a fight he would always remove his gold-rimmed glasses and give them to a noncombatant. Then he would cock his fists and do his best.

Street heroics, the acceptance of conflict and pain, fierce competitive impulses, all these evoked my wistful admiration. Yet I sensed an undercurrent of meanness in some athletes. If Budesa was a sportsman and gentleman, there were trolls and Calibans stalking the playing fields. Exposure to summer camps made me ambivalent about athletes who were something less than parfit gentle knights. Too often the star pitcher or basketball player was also a sadist, a thief, an egomaniac. Herman Wouk evidently came to the same conclusion. In his novel *The City Boy* the unathletic protagonist, Herbie Bookbinder, runs into Lennie Krieger, All-Around Camper, All-Around Athlete, a thirteen-year-old who outperforms sixteen-year-olds. Lennie is also cruel, malevolent, selfish, a bully and a liar. Yet the camp owner hails him as "the essence of character and sportsmanship."

Oh, how I lived through a series of Lennie Kriegers! How clearly I recall an adored counselor, a Big Ten halfback. He forced us to make his bed and rewarded us by stealing our sweatsocks. There was another legendary figure, a high school phenomenon, a six-letter man from upstate New York. We would try to draw him out about his sixty-yard runs and no-hit games, and he would look dully down the table and mutter, "More soup, more soup." His rudeness did not discourage us. We worshiped him.

One day in the Camp Oxford mess hall, a hush fell over the room as a group of adults entered. My counselor pointed to a broken-nosed young man among the visitors. "Kid," he said, "you want your eyes to pop out of your head? That's Al Singer, the former lightweight champion of the world." My eyes did indeed pop. *Al Singer!* The man who had won the title with a one-round knockout of Sammy Mandel, then lost it in one round to Tony Canzoneri! He was a god, a figure of wonder and awe. We gave him a standing ovation. Years later I read of his death in the *Times*. Nothing seemed to have worked for him after he lost his crown. Obscure jobs, drifting. But I had seen him once in a camp mess hall, flat-nosed, shaking his clasped hands over his head.

"Be a he-man," my father used to say. But I grew up tall, formless, uncoordinated, unable to throw a punch, and in terror of receiving one. In dread of humiliation, I held back. It's hard to say what depressed me more—my mother's cautionary advices to beware of fights, Negroes, and automobiles or my father's insistence on the need for boxing lessons, which both of us knew would never materialize. (In dreams I saw myself in Ben Lee or Everlast shorts, bouncing nimbly on high-laced shoes, a classy welterweight inviting comparisons with Georgie Abrams.)

Early on I realized that I lacked not only athletic talent but also the attitudes that make a winner. Contests were entered with a premonition of defeat. One year I managed to play—reasonably well, a centerfielder who made some memorable catches—with an intramural softball team at Columbia that got to the finals. But in the big game, against a fraternity team loaded with jocks, I was ingloriously called out on strikes with the winning run on base. To this day my tennis is soft and hesitant. When I win it is only because my middle-aged opponents determinedly go for hard winners that find the net or the back court. I never taunt my ad-

versary, never try to psych him. What if he tries to do it to me?
He'll succeed. The big choke will rise in my chest, clot my throat,
force me to double-fault.

Something additional must be said about my undergraduate
years at Columbia in the late 'thirties and early 'forties. How to
phrase it? Perhaps it is easiest to say that Columbia softened my
view of athletes. They did not all require worship. Nor were they
necessarily selfish louts, stealers of sweatsocks, indifferent to the
lesser breeds who adored them. By and large, Columbia football
players were sober pre-meds and engineers. Columbia halfbacks
and tackles became obstetricians, geologists, educators. One outstanding Columbia quarterback showed his good taste when, as
an Assistant Secretary of the Treasury, he fired G. Gordon Liddy.

These men, of course, had the best of two worlds, and I always
envied them for it. Cerebral and muscular, they seemed to have
managed to come close to the Greek ideal. Many of them were,
and remain, my close friends. But the truth is that I sensed thirty
years ago and indeed sense today an invisible barrier between us.
They competed; took blows; hit back. They did not run from
fights. I will be forever convinced that they have some mystical
edge on me, can boast of achievements I will never know. When
a group of old Columbia athletes gathers at alumni functions I
find myself listening, silent and respectful, still an outsider.

Perhaps I overstate the case. The quarterbacks and guards of
my youth, balding and paunchy today, do not seem that impressed with past glories. "Why did I waste all that time playing football?" a former Columbia captain asked rhetorically at a
party some months ago. The man is now the chief attending physician in internal medicine at a great hospital complex. "Waste!"
he went on. "I hated the game, I hated the contact, it ruined my
knees for golf and tennis, and the scholarship wasn't even worth
it." So it goes. I listen, convinced that I missed something. These
men took abuse from the legendary Lou Little, were flattened by
Michigan and Georgia blockers, and lived to talk about it.

Do I exaggerate the whole business? Probably. We're all Mittyesque dreamers, we Americans past forty, forever soothing ourselves with visions of a last-minute touchdown pass, a winning basket at the buzzer. My own sense of deprivation may be a bit greater than most, and a bit more bizarre. Forbidden by my mother to ride a two-wheeled bicycle, ice skate, or roller skate— I was not even allowed to join the Boy Scouts!—I finally did learn to manage a bike.

Another memory: I'm twenty-two years old, a tall, rugged-looking fellow with a long, bald head and calm eyes. I'm a sergeant in the United States Army, Ordnance Department. We are in the company street of the 827th Ordnance Base Depot Company, in cold, muddy Cheltenham, England. Captain Messner, my nemesis, a prissy man who looks like an impotent Errol Flynn, turns to me and orders: "Sergeant, jump on that bicycle and take this message to battalion headquarters."

It's my moment of truth. There, in front of 110 ridgerunners and big-city hoods, I blurt out: *"Sir, I cannot ride a bike."* My shame is so total, so self-damning, that not a man among those Kentucky riflemen and Chicago gunsels laughs or mocks me. Captain Messner turns aside. He cannot look at my face. I am like a diseased animal.

Alone in the company street, my feet nailed to the duckboards, I am rescued by Pfc. Benny Chavez of Albuquerque, New Mexico. Kind, good Benny! He was a tent-mate, a squat, round, brown, black-eyed man of infinite patience and good humor. "I will teach you how to ride," he says softly. He borrows a bicycle from the company rack, shoves me on, steadies me, wheels me around—and has me riding in five minutes. "Jesus Chris'," I can hear Benny Chavez saying, "look at that crazy guy go! Steady, steady, man." It was sublimely easy. How facilely I conquered fear! In a day or two I had become the Riding Fool of the 827th, speeding in and out of warehouses, riding "nunnies," sidesaddle, backward. I pedaled past Captain Messner's astonished eyes so often he made me Official Depot Messenger. That night I wrote to my mother explaining that, although I loved her, I had learned to ride a bike. My children, years later, rode two-wheelers at five, skied and ice-skated at six, were on horses at seven. In her teens, my daughter climbed mountains in Switzerland, with pitons, crampons, and a Swiss boyfriend. Often I wonder, where is Benny Chavez? And does he know he is as much of a hero to me as Sid Luckman was?

The point of all this is that fear, timidity, and ineptitude can in some degree be overcome. Not entirely. Not always. But we do rise above our limitations—real or imagined—and even if the act of rising is minimal, laughable, and arbitrary, it's worth the effort. We all seem to suffer these *lacunae* in our lives. (At least we *think* we do.) On cold winter nights I remember Benny Chavez and the day I rode the bike, and I promise myself I will not double-fault at set point again.

Some years ago I told the Benny Chavez story to a friend of mine named Jack Arbolino. Athlete and scholar, Arbolino epitomizes to me what a balanced, sane, creative man should be. In his youth he was a football player and a Marine hero. In his fifties, he is still a champion at handball. No one ever threw fiercer blocks, and no man I know is more understanding and compassionate.

"I don't comprehend football," I said, after telling him how Benny Chavez got me on a bike. "There's David out there getting blasted every week, full of bruises, sprains, taking crap from the coaches. Why does he do it?"

"You get used to it," Arbolino said. "Besides, he's young."

"Marie thinks he does it to make up for my failings."

Arbolino shook his head. "What I know of Dave, he has his own mind. So what? So he knows you have migraine headaches and colds all the time."

"It's more than that." Over lunch I choke out the story of my frustrated boyhood. It all comes out: deprived of roller skating, ice skating, a two-wheeler, I'm like a character in an Odets play, the one who keeps bemoaning his lost youth with gems like *"When I was a boy, the janitor's son had freckles all over his arms. . . ."*

Jack Arbolino leans over the table. His broad face is full of Mediterranean wisdom. "Want to know something? I can't either."

"Can't what?"

"Ice skate, roller skate, ride a bike."

"But you . . . tough Italian kid from the Bronx. You . . ."

"It's true. My mother thought I had weak ankles. At fifteen I was playing sandlot football with twenty-year-old men in Van Cortlandt Park. Paul Governali, who was fourteen, and I were the stars. But I couldn't ride a bike and I still can't."

So I was not alone. Jack, a hero of Tarawa and Saipan, also lived under the curse of presumed weak ankles. Oh, but he had paid his dues in other ways: the Marines, football. In my fifties, I'm still not a real American. Hemingway laughed as he shot hyenas in their guts. Mailer cocks his right, jabs smartly with his left. And me? Well, I don't fear dogs, but I am certain every police car on the Merritt Parkway is looking for me.

All right, Dos Passos wrote after Sacco and Vanzetti were executed, *two Americas.* (Strange, how he ended up with the *other* America.) There *are* two Americas, and on many levels. There are New Yorkers, for example, and everybody else. And there are those who stick and those who don't. As my son's football career reached dizzy summits, I plunged, vicariously of course, into the sticking camp.

Another college memory, another friend. A man named Joe Kertz, a red-faced, broken-nosed senior at Columbia. He was older than the rest of us. Kertz, of German-Irish descent, street-tough, had worked his way through Columbia over a six-year period, earning his tuition as a Con Ed repairman. Like Arbolino, he possessed an admirable balance of strength and gentleness. He had been a Golden Gloves champion at seventeen and still worked out with the bags and jumped rope. He hated to fight. Years later I met him on Long Island. Soft-voiced, sad-eyed, he was a popular high school English teacher.

"Kertz will not use his fists," a friend told me one night during our college years. We were walking north on Broadway after a night of beer drinking. Kertz and two other seniors were walking ahead of us.

"Why? What if people challenge him?"

"He talks his way out. He says he's hit enough people in his time. He just wants to teach English."

At the corner of West 113th Street and Broadway, a crowd was watching a stout man beating a young woman. He pounded her with flat, inexpert blows. She made whinnying sounds and, instead of running or appealing for help, clutched at his flailing arms, grabbed for his neck. No one tried to stop him or call a policeman.

"Hey," Joe Kertz said. "Stop hitting her."

"Go fuck yourself," the man gasped. "She's a whore."

"That doesn't give you any right to hit her," Kertz said. "Now cut it out."

"I'll hit *you,* you goddamn college boy."

The man staggered toward Kertz, puffing, gobbling chunks of warm air. He swung once and missed. Later none of us could recall seeing Kertz throw a punch. But he must have done so, and we understood why he detested violence and felt no urge to provoke fights. The man was crumbling slowly, like a building detonated from the basement. The middle of his face seemed to have been split by an axe. The upper lip was cut to the gums and teeth. Someone appeared to have drawn a thick crimson smear down his nose, mouth, and chin. We ran all the way to the dormitories. No one spoke to Kertz. He seemed upset.

I'd known it for all of my boyhood, but that hot night on Broadway, when I was eighteen, I understood that I would always be an alien in a world of violent men. Not for me the face-off on a dusty street in a Western town. Secretly I questioned my own Americanism, nurtured the possibility that I was something less than a man. My younger son must have had inklings of this whenever he threw a block or made a tackle.

2

An evening in early September. I'm phoning the *Stamford Advocate* to see if they have the score of the King–St. Luke's game. David has forbidden me to attend. King will surely be slaughtered. He doesn't want me pacing the sidelines, my long face drooping with misery, shouting shrill encouragements to his white-jerseyed team. The *Advocate* has no information. My newspapering days should have told me: It's an afternoon paper. At night the office must be all but empty.

I hear the old Buick groaning into the driveway. Seconds later, dragging his duffle bag, David enters.

"Well?" I asked.

"We got murdered."

"Badly?"

"Nah. Sixty-two to six."

He slumps into a kitchen chair. He is talking strangely, as if reading speed-writing. There is a shortage of vowels, a slurring of consonants.

"Are you hurt?" Marie asks. "You look hurt."

"Mr. Stnley thnks I hv a cncssion."

"Oh my God!" she cries. "I hate football. I hate the way you make him play it."

"Ma, nbdy makes me play ftbl."

33

"Where does it hurt? What happened?" I am studying his bruised brown face. The jaw is not moving properly.

"Nthing. It was the last ply of the game. Steve Smith rn ovr me."

"Intentionally!" Marie screams. "He did it on purpose!"

"Ma, Steve is frnd of mine. He stk me."

I am on my feet prowling the kitchen, staring at my son. He has been through the fiery furnace and survived. He has earned his purple heart. I am walking by my son's side through the world I never made. Then I see his hands. They are like lumps of uncooked beef.

"Your hands?" I ask. "What . . . ?"

"Sore. Plyed whole gme."

Marie, eyes blazing with anger, fear, horror, is staring at his face. "Why can't you talk? What happened to your voice?"

"Ma, Chrssake, lv me alone. I got smked in the jaw. Last play of the game. Jesus, lv me alone."

"Then eat something. Here, I made a steak."

David looks dolefully at the sirloin. "Can't mv my jaw." He sits motionless at the kitchen table.

Caesar, our dim-brained Golden Retriever, waddles in and lays his furry head in David's lap. He knows. He suffers with him.

"Did you tackle Siganos?" I asked anxiously.

"Cple of times. Waved at him rst of the day."

"You are dreadful," my wife says to me. "The boy has a concussion. He can't move his jaw. He can barely speak. He can't eat. His hands are deformed. *And all you want to know is if he tackled Siganos!*"

"It's important. Dave, how bad do you feel? Did Buzz Stanley look you over after you got hurt?"

"Asked me my nme. Who we plyd. Score. As if I cd frgt the score. Jsus, sixty-two to six."

"And he thought you had a concussion?" Marie asks.

"Nt rlly. Maybe."

Marie groans. What kind of an Italian is she? Her people produced Joe DiMaggio, Jake LaMotta, Phil Esposito. They know pain, violence, anger. Why is she so upset? Have I infected her with my Talmudical timidity, my bred-in-the-bone fear of getting hurt?

"Siganos as good as they say he is?" I ask. "Does he hit hard?"

"Fst. Made me blv. He's got nine-five spd."

Marie is on the phone trying to raise a local doctor. It is Saturday night, a lost cause. At last she calls New York—Mel Hershkowitz, old friend, Columbia classmate. He is one of the rare adults in the world who can talk to young people on equal terms.

Marie explains what is wrong with Dave—the frozen jaw, the slurred speech, the loss of appetite, the mutilated hands.

"Dave?" Mel asks. "Are you dizzy?"

"No. He dnt ht me that hrd."

"Your jaw is sore?"

"A ltl."

"No appetite?"

"I'm hngry as hll. But I can't mv teeth."

"Vision okay? You hear me clearly?"

Dave is getting annoyed. He cannot stand the fussing. "Yeah, yeah. I'm fine. My mthr is drvng me nuts, Mel."

"Get a good night's sleep and if you're dizzy or can't see well or hear well in the morning call me. What was the score?"

"It was clse. Sixty-two to six."

"Well, maybe next week."

Marie and I speak briefly to Mel. David struggles to get up. His thick body is battered and exhausted. Not just the ravaged hands and the immobile jaw. He drags himself upstairs. Caesar pads behind him. He will remain in David's room all night, fouling the air with his bad breath and his rank coat, dumb, worshipful, adoring.

"He sounds okay," Mel says. "That's the trouble with prep school football, the disparity in size and talent. They have kids weighing one-forty blocking on kids who weigh two-fifty."

"And more," I babble. "The star lineman on St. Luke's is a boy named Griffiths. A mere two hundred and sixty-eight pounds. Dave

had to block on him. Can you imagine?" A lunatic note of ex-
hilaration is shivering my voice.

"It's wrong," Mel says. "But if that's what he wants . . ."

"Dave is rugged."

"You're insane," Marie interrupts. "You're living *his* football,
and I hate it. I hate the game and I hate the way you react to it."

"He'll be all right," Mel says. "He needs a rest."

We return to the dinner table. The steak is cold. "You infuriate
me," Marie says. "You're wallowing in that boy's misery."

"I admit it."

"You're proud of his concussion."

"He doesn't have one."

"You sat there glorying in David's smashed jaw, the way his
hands were torn apart. All because your mother wouldn't let you
play in the street when you were little."

"It's harmless. Give me my small pleasures."

Upstairs I hear the noise of the Allman Brothers on David's
record player. Caesar will soon join in with some well-tuned
howls. Music to ease the pain of defeat.

"They shouldn't have scheduled St. Luke's," I say, trying to
change the subject. "They're the terrors of the league. Mike Siganos is the greatest running back in the history of the Fairchester
League. They have huge linemen, giant blocking backs. Half the
Fairchester teams refused to play them."

"And King? The worst team in the league? What are they doing
playing St. Luke's?"

"I'll have to ask Buzz. It's an interesting question. Dave told
me before the season that he was afraid of only two teams—St.
Luke's and Hackley. They could handle anyone else."

"Don't you understand anything? That's our son up there with
what might be a fractured jaw. And you're talking about the
schedule."

But I hear her only dimly over the sounds of the phonograph.
Dave went down in glory. *The last play of the game* and he was
still sticking. Steve Smith. Mike Siganos. Fat Charlie Griffiths.

The elite of the league. And Dave hitting to the bitter end. I would have given up after five minutes. *Two* minutes.

"It could have been worse," I say.

"Really?"

"Sure. They scored, didn't they? Last week Rye beat King forty-two to nothing. St. Luke's is a better team. King got on the scoreboard. They may turn the whole thing around before the season is over. I'm going to every game from now on. I should have been there today."

Later I look in on Dave. The record player is blaring rock music. He is in a stupefied sleep in his street clothes. He breathes noisily. The aggrieved jaw looks peaceful enough, but his red, swollen hands are crossed on his chest. Is he dreaming of Fat Charlie leveling him, of Mike Siganos running over him? And has he any idea of how, with each game, he is redeeming something for a foolish father?

Buzz Stanley hears I'm working on a book about the King season and invites me to look at the St. Luke's films. "It wasn't as bad as the score indicates," Buzz says. "We played them even for a quarter. I had Dick Whitcomb, the St. Luke's coach, climbing a tree. It was only six-nothing at the end of the quarter, and he was talking to himself trying to crank something up against us."

"But the final score—sixty-two to six?"

"Everything came apart," Buzz shakes his handsome head. "God, I really thought we could win that game."

I am transported back twenty-odd years. My friend Paul Governali, once an All-American back at Columbia, later with the New York Giants, is working as a backfield coach for Lou Little. I am at Paul's house for dinner after a Columbia-Army game at West Point. Final score: Army 63, Columbia 12. And I remember Paul's dark, somber, sad-eyed face as he says to me, almost weeping, over and over, "It could have gone the other way . . . we started out great . . . had them on the run . . . then something happened . . ."

Coaches have to think that way, I suppose. It is surely a better attitude than mine. I enter all contests, whether it be pick-up mixed doubles or a game of HORSE in our backyard basketball court, convinced that I will lose. No such doubts ever shiver Buzz Stanley or his captain, David Nicholas Green. "Don't play the game if you don't think you can win," Dave says. And Buzz, telling me about Dave's disgust after missing a tackle (on Siganos, who else?) and being benched. "Goddammit," Buzz shouts at him. "Suck up your guts, stop sniveling, and get back in there."

But coaches must believe. They would not go forth weekend after weekend against the St. Luke'ses of the world if they did not. A case in point: Buzz Stanley, Robert William Stanley III. He is thirty years old, born in New Rochelle, a legendary running back at Portchester High School, Brighton Academy, Wake Forest. His father played guard for Princeton. Buzz is built like a medium tank. He is 5′ 9″ and weighs 215 pounds. At Wake Forest, before torn ligaments and cartileges ended his career after a sensational sophomore year, he played fullback at a trim 200. He remained with the squad as a sort of extra coach and tutor to the other players. He worshiped his coach at Wake Forest, Cal Stall, now the head coach at the University of Minnesota.

"Football is the last thing in society that requires total dedication and discipline," Buzz tells me at lunch one day. "Paradoxically, it also demands a great deal of flexibility in individuals. A boy will give me more because he knows I appreciate this. But at the bottom line, there's only one way to judge the kids who play football. They have to like to stick."

Buzz is dark and large-headed, with an awesome neck and a massive chest. I notice a marked facial resemblance to Jerry Quarry, the heavyweight. In the King School gym I have seen him pick up a basketball and, barely looking at the hoop, toss in a perfect jump shot. He has a B.A. and an M.A. from Wake Forest and a dozen albums full of clippings. In Westchester and Fairfield counties he is a well-known figure among coaches and officials. He serves on every committee and association of coaches in the area.

His wife is a charming girl of Italian ancestry, like Marie. "She settled me down," Buzz says. "Gave me a lot of values I needed." At King School he is athletic director, football coach, and basketball coach, and he also runs the summer camp.

The 8 mm images flicker on the screen in Buzz's cramped office. Dave is watching with us, along with Andy Levison, co-captain Paul LeBlanc, and a few other boys. How pleasant can it be to review one's destruction? But they joke, sip Cokes, accept Coach Stanley's abuse and praise with remarkable calm.

"First quarter," Buzz says. "We humiliated them. Dick Whitcomb was talking to himself. He couldn't believe we were putting it to him."

We watch the ghostly images on the tiny screen—King in white uniforms and maroon helmets, St. Luke's in maroon jerseys, dark pants. I keep looking for Dave's special white helmet in the middle of the line. He is playing linebacker and defensive end.

"Look at that," Buzz says. "They couldn't do a thing. Williams fumbles for St. Luke's and recovers. Look at Siganos block on Dave. Williams gets creamed by Barrett."

Mark Barrett? A small, shy boy. The program lists him at 145 pounds. He weighs closer to 130.

There is a melee on the screen. Fat Charlie Griffiths is belting Andy Levison. They are swinging furiously. Fat Charlie has a 50-pound edge on Andy. The ref stops it and penalizes St. Luke's fifteen yards.

"They were after me," Andy says, "Bobby Fieber and me. We quit St. Luke's to go to King, and they said they'd get us."

"Lucky for Fieber he hadn't gone out for the team," I offer.

Silence. Fieber's absence is a sore point. By far the best runner in the school—big, fast, determined—he has chosen to play soccer instead of football. He is one of four or five outstanding prospects who refused to come out for the team. The previous year King was unable to field a varsity team for the first time in its history. Shame shrouded the school. Stanley had twelve men he could count on. The schedule was canceled. A haphazard junior varsity

team was put together and lost every game of a shortened schedule. This year football is in disrepute. Even the cheerleaders of
Low-Haywood are deserting them. By majority vote, they opt to
cheer for the soccer team and let the football players do their own
locomotives. ("Who needs them?" Dave growls. "Nobody knows
the cheers anyway.")

"Watch this," Buzz says, running the stop-and-go projector.
"Cam Sillars turns left end for three yards. But Chris Sweet can't
do it on third and five. We try the fake punt, but Boe drops the
pass. St. Luke's ball."

Mike Siganos trips on his own man. He is the stuff of which
myths are made. I can never get it straight. Is he five nine with
nine-five speed? Or is he nine five with five-nine speed? Last year
his average gain from scrimmage was 16.8 yards. He is bound for
Kentucky. "Greatest football player in the history of the league,"
Stanley says. Homage to an opponent. "Get the stats right: It's
four-five for the forty, nine-seven for the hundred. He can run all
day."

Incredible. King is stopping the St. Luke's offense. John Eginton, a linebacker, sticks Siganos. Dave and Eginton, blitzing linebackers, bump Balasz, the St. Luke's quarterback. Siganos catches
a pass out of bounds. St. Luke's cannot move the ball.

"By God, just look at that," Buzz says. "For ten minutes we did
to them what no other team did until they lost to Cheshire. We
could have won that game."

Andy and Dave exchange glances. I say nothing. The optimism
of coaches is one of the few pure things left in the world. I dare
not question Buzz.

"Chris Kelly was in back of their film unit. He could hear Whit-
comb on the walky-talky. Didn't know what we'd hit him with.
No, he kept saying, try something else. That won't work. No good.
That tickled me, even though Dick is one of my best friends."

Suddenly St. Luke's scores. The midget figures on the screen
face one another. Balasz fades, throws. Effortlessly, Siganos

catches the pass and scores a touchdown. Worse, he beats Dave for the score. But what is the linebacker doing covering the fastest receiver? Where are the defensive backs?

"He beat your ass, buddy," Buzz says.

"Not on the extra point," Dave says.

He's right. Siganos goes in once, is called back for offside. Again, Siganos tries to turn an end. He battles past Eginton. Dave sticks him. Siganos fumbles. No extra point. Pride warms my chest like a heating pad on a torn muscle. *Once he stopped Siganos.* A man could spend a lifetime reading books and never know the thrill of sticking Mike Siganos.

King won't quit. They hold St. Luke's two more times. The 4-3 zone is working. Dave's outside rush stops a run by Steve Smith. St. Luke's punts. But King is not generating an offense. They need Bobby Fieber. Jimmy Wilson, their sophomore quarterback, looks frail. His passes don't quite reach their destination, and the pass blocking is meager. Still, King is carrying the game to the monsters, the Fat Charlies, the Siganoses, the Steve Smiths. Jimmy Wilson hits Esposito with a short pass. Espo is gang-tackled by six Lukemen. Sillars goes off tackle for five. Chris Sweet, King's freshman fullback (6', 220), goes for two more. ("The gentlest kid in the world," Buzz says wonderingly. "Hasn't got his full growth yet. After practice he baby-sits with my two kids.")

The first quarter ends and it's only 6-0, St. Luke's. Across the field, Dick Whitcomb is holding his head. How are those slobs (who didn't even field a team the year before) holding us?

"Six to zip at the quarter." Buzz shakes his head. "It was damn near a victory."

"Second quarter coming up," says Andy Levison.

Dave says: "They scored thirty-four or thirty-six points. Twenty-eight points in three minutes. I waved at Siganos when he ran past me." His speech is thick. His jaw is still sore two days after the game.

The screen becomes a blur of dark jerseys racing into the King end zone. Siganos takes a kick and flies seventy-eight yards for a touchdown. The floodgates have opened. Seconds later, Steve Smith is running twenty-six yards for anther score.

"Your fault, Mean Joe," Buzz grumbles.

Dave shades his eyes. On the screen against the St. Luke's monsters, his meanness is hard to discern.

"Some linebacker," Buzz goes on. He reverses the action, runs the play in slow motion so we can see David's shame. "You were sucked in. Went left when you should have gone right. Smith suckered you."

Fat Charlie keeps kicking off for St. Luke's—thunderous, arching kicks. They are like blows to my heart. "What a guy," Levison says. "He came to training weighing two hundred and eighty-eight pounds. Whitcomb made him lose weight, so now he's only two-sixty-eight."

Fat Charlie is blocking on poor Sillars—Sillars, with his pale face, surprised eyes, skinny limbs. Cam goes down as if leveled by a heavy wrecker. He looks as if he will never rise.

Jimmy Wilson, our slender quarterback, is buried and fumbles. St. Luke's recovers. On the next play, Siganos races twenty-two yards. Not a hand is laid on him. David makes a desperate lunge, misses by yards.

"Jesus," Buzz moans. "He didn't even bother to cut, just kept running. That's what he thought of you."

The St. Luke's scoreboard looks like a cash register in a supermarket. I am reminded of Harpo Marx in his chariot, dumping footballs into the opponent's end zone in *Horse Feathers*. When I mention it, I get no laugh.

Sam Boe gets his chance at quarterback. King uses a strange formation, with Boe dropping back for a direct snap from center before passing. It's Stanley's invention. Boe is barely able to raise his arm before a wave of dark jerseys drowns him.

"Poor guy," Andy Levison says. "He didn't know whether to laugh or cry. He was in the huddle, shaking, giggling, ready to bawl. He'd drop, we'd collapse, and six guys would lie on him."

The score is 38-0. But King's defense is still trying. Dave stunts, crashes, tackles Steve Smith, who Buzz tells me will probably play for Army next year. On the next play Dave blitzes and is fooled, as the play goes the other way.

"Oh, they wanted to run it up," Buzz says. "It was homecoming day. King used to be the jock school around here. Now it's St. Luke's."

On the next play, Dave and Gary LeBlanc (no relation to the King center, Paul "Rag" LeBlanc) collide, almost square off. Le-Blanc (6' 2", 210) doesn't appreciate being hit by a 175-pound linebacker. I know about LeBlanc. Whitcomb has told me he might be a prospect for Columbia.

A few plays later, in the gray silence, I see Gary LeBlanc smash into David and level him, so that Steve Smith can walk over him. But they're stopped at the goal line. St. Luke's doesn't score again as the half ends. It's 38-0.

"A few breaks and we might have had them," Buzz says. He means it.

There have been some injuries. Scott Osman has had his face torn open by Balasz's cleats. He needs stitches, will be out for the season. He's a good defensive back.

"For God's sake, why did you schedule these guys?" I ask, as we await the second half.

"To keep the league going," the coach explains. "To save King football. After not fielding a varsity team, we had to stand up and be counted. Brunswick dropped us because they were afraid we wouldn't have a team for a second year. Whitcomb knew he was loaded so he scheduled a lot of tough nonleague opponents—Milburn, Cheshire. But we decided it was important that the Big Four of the Fairchester League all play—King, Brunswick, Hackley and St. Luke's. Hamden Hall, Rye, and New York School for the Deaf don't play everyone."

"Still . . ." I am the old cautionary scorekeeper. Why get murdered? Why play to be humiliated? I keep thinking of the *Advocate*'s cruel reporting. *A laugher. Hapless King School . . .*

"It was a matter of pride," Buzz says. The second half begins. "You do some things for pride."

I look at the stricken faces in the darkened office. Dave is nursing his jaw. Andy Levison is solemn. Pale Cam Sillars. Big Rutledge. Do they agree with Buzz's decision? They must. But I learn that after the first game, when Rye, supposedly not much better than King, drubbed them 42-0, Dave had called Buzz for some philosophical talk. *Is it worth it?* my son had asked. To go out and be slaughtered by Siganos and company? "Don't play if you don't think you can win," Buzz said sternly. "We can beat those guys."

I also learn what motivated that call. David is not the kind of boy to make appeals. "I called Buzz because Cameron Sillars had just called me," he confesses. "He was fed up with football after Rye killed us. The jayvees lost every game the year before. He was disgusted. So I called Mr. Stanley."

Who is right? Who knows better? Were the four or five good football players who chose *not* to go out for the team smarter than David and Andy? Are we forever required to show our *machismo*, flaunt our capacity for pain and hurt? If we are, then I can only see my son and his brave teammates—Levison, Eginton, Rutledge, all of them suffering annihilation, taking their lumps—as small heroes.

On the sidelines, a man in a windbreaker is trailing Buzz as the St. Luke's second string continues to run up the score. The coach reverses the film, stops the action. "Who's that guy?" he asks.

"It's Mr. Fieber," Andy says.

"Oh, yeah," Buzz shakes his head. "Now I remember. He was on my tail all through the second half, giving me advice. I'd huddle with Kelly and Sample, and there'd be this guy telling me what defense to use." He laughs. "And his kid, the best runner in the school, isn't playing for me."

Coppola, number 14, a sub for Siganos, runs past David for long yardage. It's 44-0. David nails him when he tries for the extra point. But then Coppola scores again. It's 50-0.

I see someone who looks like a midget tackle a St. Luke's back twice his size.

"Who's that?" I ask.

"Mori," Dave says. "Mike Mori."

"How big?"

"The program says he's one-fifteen," Andy says. "But the Little Wimp weighs a hundred and one. He loves to stick."

I am stunned. "One hundred and one pounds? Against people like Fat Charlie at two-sixty-eight?" There is something hideously wrong about his kind of football.

"We were looking for people who like to hit," Buzz explains patiently. "Mike Mori likes to hit. Look at him belt that guy."

"That's the Little Wimp," Paul LeBlanc says.

Perhaps Mori's 101-pound courage inspires King. They are marching for a touchdown. One of Buzz's hipper-dipper plays works. Ralph Esposito, the tight end, takes a hand-off from Jimmy Wilson, drops back. Boe sprints downfield, catches a forty-yard pass. Sillars is running well—three yards, eight, again for three. Dave leads the blocking.

"They didn't want us to score," Dave says. "I could hear them. *Stop 'em, stop the bastards*, they were saying."

From the six-yard line, Sillars, a pale ghost, drifts in for the touchdown. It's 50-6. I am shivering. Each hard yard of turf, each block, has been like blood drawn from an open vein.

Twice more St. Luke's scores. They do it effortlessly, running over and around the exhausted King kids. Even on the screen, his figure shadowy, vague, my son looks weary.

"Poor Boe," Andy says. "He got his glasses knocked off almost every time."

"He came of age in this game," Buzz says. "He became a man. He learned how to get hit."

Final play of the game: Oldford, St. Luke's all-league center, tries to blow David out on an off-tackle play. He misses, but Steve Smith, carrying in an attempt to hit 70 points, collides with David. I see my son spin around, bend, go down. Smith runs over his flattened form but is stopped. No score.

"Isn't that beautiful," Buzz murmurs, as the film runs out. "Smith belts Dave high, Oldford low, Smith steps on his crotch, runs up his spine, and kicks him in the jaw. That's how football should be played."

The screen is blank. So is my mind. No wonder David's jaw was immobilized.

"It didn't hurt," he mumbles. "Not for long anyway."

"Last play of the game?" I ask. "To get blasted on a meaningless last play?"

"I dug my helmet into him," Dave says. "But he had the better angle."

The street wisdom of my youth maintained that there was always an angle, or, in Brooklyn parlance, "a nangle." Evidently such is the case in sticking. And failure to have an angle, or a better one, can result in a stiff jaw and fractured speech.

The screen goes dark. We await the dire Saturdays to come, my son and I, his body bruised, my spirit shivering.

3

As I age I seem to recall the past largely in terms of summers. Oh, I can recollect an interesting autumn now and then, a worthwhile spring (winters are a blur of head colds, skids on icy roads), but the summers return to my mind's eye clear, hard-outlined, full of Perugino blues and El Greco reds and Fra Angelico greens.

Maybe two years of residence in Italy have filled my marbled mind with these bright images. If you say to me "1971," I see an August day when Marie and I walked into a small museum in Borgo Sansepolcro. Alone in the cool plaster chamber we stood awed by a dozen of the greatest Piero Della Francescas in the world.

How about 1944? Easy. I was in England with the 827th Ordnance Base Depot company. The Shakespeare Festival at Stratford. Stacking truck tires in a Nissen hut. A lovely English girl I knew briefly. Visits to her parents' stone farmhouse in Chipping Campden, a house that was listed in the Domesday Book and had runic characters incised in the hearthstones.

1954? A split-level house in Westbury, Long Island. My older son, Ted, just born. My neighbor Morty Jaffe taking me out on a fishing boat owned by a friend known to me only as "Frank the Gambler." They get me staggering drunk in celebration of the birth of my first son. A four-day migraine follows. I become a teetotaler.

Over all, 1973 was a fair summer. It started well, ended in confusion. All three children were at home, a mixed bag affording
us mixed blessings. Our daughter, Nancy, having fulfilled her required half-year of college dropout, is working as a waitress at
Rico's Restaurant in Stamford prior to returning to Brandeis for
her senior year. Nancy is intense, hard-working, yeasty, articulate. The owners of Rico's, speaking thick Neapolitan Italian, are
rendered sullenly confused by her. Not that she is not a good
waitress. She is fast, smart, knows her *parmigiana* from her *caccia-
tore*. But she speaks better Italian than they do—Tuscan Italian,
learned when she was a child in Italy and later refined in an in-
tensive course at Brandeis. (Who ever heard of anyone going to
Brandeis to learn Italian? Ugaritic, Chaldean, Aramaic, okay. But
Italian?)

"Hey, Nance," the boss would ask. "Where ya learn to speak
such Eye-talian?"

"I lived in Italy."

"Ya lyin."

Nancy shrugs, shouts an order to the cook. The cook likes her.
He is from north of Rome and can appreciate good grammar. But
the owners look at her with clouded eyes. To them she is as mysterious as Garibaldi was to the peasants of Sicily. She leaks word
to them that she is only half-Italian. Her father is Jewish. There
are long, sinister pauses. The brothers and cousins who own
Rico's now regard her as nothing short of a *strega*, a witch, a
conjurer.

Angelo, one of the entrepreneurs, takes her aside and in a
throaty voice asks, "So if ya Jewish, how come ya workin' as a
waitress?"

Ted, my older boy, takes summer courses at the Stamford
branch of the University of Connecticut. He does this to avoid
morning classes at Columbia, where he helps edit the *Spectator*,
studies "film," and sleeps a great deal. He spends hours going
through the Columbia curriculum in search of courses that begin
at 2 P.M. or later. The summer courses at Connecticut give him a

chance of getting rid of requirements, widening the field for intense afternoon study. In his spare time, that summer of '73, he works as a uniformed guard for Gleason Security, punching a time-clock, making the rounds at places like Olin, Executone, Timex. Thus does corporate America take care of the children of its sworn enemies—media villains like myself. The Gleason supervisors like Ted. He is dependable, quiet, intelligent. But they make him get rid of his beard. "Wouldn't look right, Ted," Mr. Hill, the chief security officer, says. Marie worries about the boy, but the job suits him perfectly. He works nights, reads, does his school work, and can sleep all day.

My wife is finishing her master's degree at Fairfield University in 1973. She has discovered with delight that the Jesuits with whom she takes courses in Learning Disabilities are liberals, even radicals, light years removed from the hard-fisted coreligionists she knew as a child in the Bronx. Generously, she informs a fair young Jesuit: "Father, if the priests were like you when I was a girl, you wouldn't have lost me. But the Irish always made Italians feel like second-class Catholics."

He smiles at her. "There's still a chance, Marie." But he doesn't force the issue.

In all, a summer of work and progress. David, not yet seventeen, has finished his junior year at King, that grim no-football year. Buzz Stanley hires him as tennis coach for the King School day camp. The job is a plum. Four or five boys have been competing for it. He will coach tennis all day and drive a rattling green-and-white camp bus. He will earn $600 for a summer's work.

Then one day the news breaks. Dave has been elected co-captain of the King football team. The other co-captain is the tight end, Scott Davidson. Old Weak Ankles cannot believe the grand news. *A football captain? In our home? In our time?* A football-captain son for the man who lost almost all of his fights?

"What kind of a team will you have?" I ask.

"Terrific. A great line. We need a few backs and ends."

Ancient fears shiver my bowels. A school that could not field a team the year before. A junior varsity that lost all its games.

"Mr. Stanley says we should be six and two. Except for Hackley and St. Luke's, we can play everyone even."

"Where will he play you?"

"Linebacker, I guess. Guard on offense. I call defensive signals."

My cup runneth over. My good fortune cannot be believed. After all the books read, papers written, A's recorded, degrees attained, we have a football captain in the house.

"What weight will you be for the season?"

"Oh, one-eighty, one-seventy-five. Mr. Stanley wants me to have some speed. It doesn't matter. He'll list me at one-ninety-one in the program no matter what I weigh."

Pessimist that I am, I sense rumblings of disaster as early as July. Scott Davidson quits the team. I hear Dave making pained appeals to his co-captain on the phone. Davidson won't play. He has injured his head in a diving accident and has no desire to stick and get stuck.

Paul LeBlanc, a junior, the team center, a tall, calm boy, is named to succeed Davidson. LeBlanc has a confident look. They call him "Rag" for reasons that I can guess at but are never revealed to me.

But there are other no-shows. David Dwelle, the best passer in King School, resists Dave's blandishments. He doesn't want to play football either. John Daum, the best pass receiver, prefers to play soccer, along with little Peter Fisher, the breakaway runner I remember so poignantly from the sixth and seventh grades.

The most grievous loss of all is Bobby Fieber. Bobby is a genuine 190 pounds and extremely fast.

"I could make a real star out of that kid," Buzz muses to me one night. "A world of natural talent." But Fieber, according to Buzz, told him last year: "Varsity soccer looks better than jayvee football on a college application." His feelings persist to 1973.

But Buzz and Dave remain full of hope. The rest of the school seems unconvinced. How can they think of getting on the same field with St. Luke's? The very name *Siganos* makes coaches in the Fairchester League turn whiter than a sideline marker.

"Dave," I say, "can Buzz be serious? Look at who *isn't* playing. Dwelle, the best passer. Daum, the best receiver. Fieber, the best runner. Davidson, the best end."

"They're wussy," he says. "We'll have a team even without all those guys. They just don't want to play on a team that might get beat."

Wussy is also new to me. Like LeBlanc's nickname, "Rag," I can guess at the origin. I ask.

"It rhymes with something that sounds like it," my son says. "It's the same as being a candy-ass." He reaches for the phone. The great proselytizer trying to convert the heathen to *sticking*. It is a lost cause. Buzz will not deign to plead with recalcitrants. He does offer to buy a special helmet for John Daum, who, like Davidson, has a head injury. Understandably, Daum would still rather play soccer. The team will depend on backs like "Wimp" Mori at 101 pounds, Matt Gormley at 120, Jimmy Wilson at 140. There is a kind of exhilarated lunacy in the air. Finally Dave gains a recruit. He is John Tukes, a slender, bespectacled black boy.

"I really worked him over," Dave says cryptically. " 'Come on, Tukes, baby,' I said, 'you are our main man.' "

Main Man Tukes is the only one of the shrinking violets to show up for practice. A reluctant tiger, he is slight and scholarly and wants to be a disc jockey. I have the feeling he doesn't care for the game and is there merely to integrate the squad. He weighs about 140, but Buzz will list him at 165. Either Stanley is convinced that he will frighten the pants off his opponents with these inflated statistics or he can't count. I'm reminded of P. T. Barnum, or at least of Will Cuppy's observation about him. When Barnum measured Jumbo, Cuppy says, the elephant was fifteen feet high; when anyone else measured the animal, it was two feet closer to the ground.

One of the league coaches informs Buzz—who relays the story

to David—how he rates his opponents. "If I see a line-up of Italian and Polack names, I worry. If there's a lot of Jewish names, I'm not scared at all. But if they're WASP names—you know, Smith, Jones—I don't know whether to worry or not. They could be real WASPs—no worry. Or they could be black, which is plenty to worry about." Dave laughs. Buzz is delighted to discover he is half-Italian. I feel like Robert Frost at John Kennedy's inauguration, telling the President to be "more Irish than Harvard." "My boy," I find myself muttering, "be more Neapolitan than Litvak."

The summer—a lovely, serene Connecticut summer—goes its leafy, humid way. Marie and I are married twenty-three years. We worry about our growing children. We are grateful for past favors, apprehensive about the new world of shortages and scarce jobs they will face. But David is expanding—his chest and arms thickening, his black hair curling, his skin turning muddy brown. When he was an infant in Fregene, the beach resort near Rome, the attendants called him *scugnizzo*—the street urchin, gutter rat. His energy confounds me. Up at 7:30, he tools the camp bus in and out of country lanes picking up his campers. Then four hours of tennis coaching, keeping wild kids in line. Often he works evenings with Buzz, getting the rosters ready, preparing playbooks.

"Mr. Stanley found a great school for us to play," he tells me one night over dinner. "St. Hugh's of New York. They haven't won a game for three years."

I'm suspicious at once. If Buzz is scouting losers, he must be worried about the rest of the schedule. Not just awesome St. Luke's and dread Hackley, but even Rye and Hamden Hall. He must realize that without four or five of the best athletes in school —"What is wrong with those guys?" I keep asking David—and with only thirteen usable football players, he is in for a bad time.

"St. Hugh's, eh?"

"Near Columbia. They needed an away game. It's going to be our homecoming game." And he is off to play hockey. *Hockey in midsummer?* Hockey is what ruined David's tennis. Or maybe football did. Or skiing. Did I leave anything out? There was a spell of Little League baseball. Of course the coach took one look at his neck and his legs and made him a catcher. A fairly good one. But baseball was too slow. Not enough contact. In lower grades at King he wrestled. But he loves hockey more than anything. It is, he tells me, the perfect sport—speed, contact, teamwork, constant motion.

The previous winter he was scheduled to take tennis lessons several times a week at John Nogrady's school in Vista, New York. Half the time David would get to the courts, suit up, start to play, and then get an urgent summons from the Crystal Rink in Norwalk. They needed a goalie. (He gravitates toward positions of punishment—catcher, goalie, linebacker.) He was the only member of the New England Lawn Tennis Association who always carried in his car goalie pads, stick, chest protector, mask, gloves.

"And you left in the middle of the set?" I ask. I was paying for all that winter tennis.

"I'd rather play hockey. Ice time is tough."

Miserliness battles pride. *Hockey?* I cannot ice skate. I don't understand the game. After hours of explanation I'm not sure I know the difference between icing and offside. And what purpose does the blue line serve? Why is Bobby Orr so great?

"Good game?"

"They were kids from the Stamford and West Hill varsity. We won nine-two."

"You must have had a good game."

He growls, stumbles up to his room. "Thirty saves. They kept saying where'd you get that goalie?"

A week later he is again urgently summoned from the tennis courts—it is January, snowy roads, icy patches, a miserable Eastern winter—to a hockey game. He changes at Vista. A tennis player in padded blue satin shorts and red suspenders.

"Well?" I ask, when he rumbles into the house after midnight.

"They had two goalies so I played defense."

"That's not your position."

"I know. But I like to hit. We won four-three. I scored two of our goals."

For a while we sit silently in the den studying the television screen with glazed eyes. In this family of 3.8 cumulatives, published books, conferences on Learning Disabilities, the *Columbia Spectator*, we have produced a mutant, a true sport. Some genetic hanky-panky has been at work. The rest of us don't love to "hit guys." None of us sticks. ("There are too many guys on the football team who don't stick," David grumbles to me later that year. "Andy and Edge and Cam and me stick.")

What's the source of this excess of muscle, desire, resilience? My own theory is that certain potent genes from David's grandfathers eluded his parents and converged in his body. My father was a gym teacher before he became a physician. Small, powerful, broad-chested, he was of the old school of Swedish gymnasts. He could perform on the parallel bars and the rings. He was poorly coordinated for games—he never learned to hit a baseball—but he possessed enormous strength. My father-in-law, Nick Pomposelli, at seventy-eight, jogs, rides a bike, plays superb shuffleboard. At boccie he can beat anyone in Tamarac Mainlands Section Six, Fort Lauderdale. Nick the Cop always had power in his long limbs. In the navy in World War I he was a wrestling champion. Later he won marathon races and earned the nickname "Longboat," after a famous Olympic runner.

Grandfatherly genes? Possibly. And maybe a certain attitude along with them. Surely not my defeat-before-we-begin gloom or Marie's indifference to athletic contests. No wonder Buzz Stanley calls on David to lead the calisthenics, recruit the no-shows, psych the team up for the big comeback season.

"If we fail this year," Buzz says ominously before the first practice, "it means the death of football at King School, and that is a disgrace that no school can afford."

How big a disgrace? I'm tempted to tell Buzz about Bill Corum's dire prediction when the University of Chicago, after many losing seasons, abandoned football in the late 'thirties. Corum, sports columnist for the Hearst newspapers and a self-appointed arbiter of athletic matters, intoned, "I hereby predict that the name of Stagg Field will be consigned to oblivion forever." What a prophet! In 1942, in an atomic pile under the concrete stands of Stagg Field, scientists achieved America's first nuclear reaction. Pick up any history of atomic research, and you will find the reference: *Stagg Field*. So much for the oblivion that the ditching of football bestows on institutions of learning.

There is a competitive pinging in the air toward the end of summer. David not only is counseling at the camp and running off for secret hockey matches (one night a player chases what he thinks is the puck toward Dave's goal and discovers that his stick is following a black rat) but also is entered in our local tennis club tournaments. Not quite seventeen, he is a strong but erratic player. I suspect he sometimes thinks the racket is a goalie stick. Boys he used to play even when he was thirteen or fourteen now win from him. They get New England rankings and tennis scholarships while he studies Phil Esposito's moves.

In the third round David plays my friend Hal Golden, forty-six, a former vice-president of MCA, a former vice-president of ABC. I am very fond of Hal and his family, but I am dazed by the notion of my son's playing a man who was vice-president of not one but *two* companies about which authors harbor certain misgivings. (See Merle Miller's *Only You, Dick Daring.*)

It is a brilliant, sun-yellowed Sunday. A crowd at the Long Ridge Club watches the matches. Hal is a top singles player, a stalwart of the "A" team. David beats him 10-8. Abandoning his wild, smashing game, he hits deep and true, comes to meet Hal's backhand, wears him down. David is an unknown. *Who is that kid?* They all know the dandy young tennis stars in their starched shorts and white shoes and fancy rolled socks. But who is this brown, thick-legged boy in the stained shirt and torn shorts who ran Hal Golden off the court?

"Fools!" I want to shout. "That is Dave Green, who, if he would get away from that damn goalie net, stop with the useless football, the skiing, the fishing, the one-on-one, the camping, and everything else, could beat all your fancy starched players!"

Then I look at Hal's wife and children. They look stricken. He was beaten by a seventeen-year-old. An *unknown* seventeen-year-old. (David hates our club. He rarely goes.) Softy that I am, I find that I am feeling sorry for Bunny and Margery and Donald Golden. Hal is a sweet man. Why did David do this? My old failing. I fear winning. I fear losing. When I win I don't know what to do with it . . . I'm hopeless.

"You should have heard the women around me," Marie boasts. "They kept saying where did that boy came from? Look at his backhand."

"He came from a Naples gutter," I say. "And thank God."

Pride, we all know, is only a step or two before disaster. Perhaps David asked for it with his cockiness. A week later he was to play the next round. If he wins he will be in the quarter finals. His opponent is the consistent Wayne Feldman. Wayne is fifteen, five feet tall (almost five-ten with his Afro), and weighs about 110. He is a friend of David's. They played at Vista whenever Dave was not putting on his hockey clothes. They usually split. Dave can beat him by concentrating.

Ed Oosterhuis, chairman of the Tennis Committee, gets annoyed with the boys for postponing their match. (Ed is tall, bespectacled, outspoken, a Bache & Co. stockbroker.) One hot August day, Dave plays three hours of singles, showers, and, exhausted, starts off to a friend's house for a night of pool and beer. Oosterhuis tracks him down and demands that he play Wayne Feldman *that very moment* or forfeit.

Cursing, boiling, my son comes home, changes to tennis clothes again, goes out to the club and snarls at Oosterhuis: "I could have played tomorrow. I was through for the day. My game's off."

All of Bache & Co. responds: "You play now or you're out."

In my coward's heart I see doom approaching. The rage in

David is consuming him, staining his skin with angry red splotches. Wayne Feldman, hiding beneath his Afro, maddeningly consistent, full of drops and lobs and alley shots, destroys David 10-1. Thus ever did rebellion find rebuke. Luckily they play on court nine, far from the admiring crowd that cheered Dave's victory over Hal Golden. David loses two games in a row. Burning, resentful, he smashes shot after shot into the net, the fences, the trees.

Ed Oosterhuis is waiting for the boys as they come off the court. "How'd it go?" He is cheerful. Men's singles are back on schedule.

"I won ten to one," Feldman says. "Dave was off."

"Tough, Dave."

David turns his back. His face is the shade of peat moss.

"Sorry about that," Oosterhuis tries. "But you guys were two days behind schedule. The tournament must go on."

"Take your tournament," my son says, "shove it up, turn it to the right and rotate it."

The tennis chairman is silent. Later they make it up, or at least I think they do. Marie says David should not think in terms of a career with Bache.

4

A five-column headline in the *Stamford Advocate:*

FOOTBALL RETURNS TO KING SCHOOL

Under it, a three-column photograph of David and Buzz. The caption reads:

KINGPINS: Captain Dave Green and head coach Buzz Stanley are ready to rebuild football at King School after a year's absence. The duo will lead the King team in Fairchester League competition this fall.

David is smiling. His neck looks almost as thick as Buzz's, which is a 17½. They wear T-shirts, which accentuate their shoulders. Two confident young men. No fears there, buster.

The article, less encouraging, terms 1972 "the darkest year in King School football history." To Stamford, and especially to the *Advocate* sports staff, the abandonment of football is a sin against the Holy Ghost. It's a decent city, full of good people, but its insignia should be a jockstrap rampant on a field of tape. The sports section of our newspaper is the best written, most detailed, best laid out part of the *Advocate.*

"Coach Stanley is approaching the new season with a positive outlook, rebuilding the sagging football fortunes at King," the article says. Oddly, it mentions Scott Davidson as co-captain, a senior tight end who is counted on for "All-Star performance." Yet he isn't in the photo. Can this be some of Buzz's shrewd psyching, to entice Davidson back to the gridiron? The article also mentions, mysteriously, that "the status of senior Bob Fieber, a 6′ 1″, 195-pound fullback, is a question mark." As I read the story it occurs to me that it is largely about players Buzz doesn't have. David has inked lines through no fewer than eleven men on the roster. It is, by and large, an imaginary team. Buzz is trying to create a self-fulfilling prophecy. Well, he's got David. The article calls him "David 'Mean Joe' Green, a hard-nosed lineman, on whom Stanley is counting to get things together defensively on the field."

As far as I am concerned, the season is a success before a game has been played. A journalist most of my life, I know the value of good notices. David can quit right now and be ahead. At least I'll feel that way. Who'll remember the losses and frustrations? We've been in print; the illusion will last; the words will survive in scrapbooks.

Seventeen boys suit up for the first practice. Of these, only about thirteen or fourteen will ever see much playing time.

"By the end of this week, you will hate my guts," Coach Stanley tells them. I hear this from Dave and decide Buzz has to lean on them extra hard. They will need a great deal of toughening.

First day of practice: a sticky September day. The thick green fields and broad shade trees of King School—it's a beautiful school —afford no solace.

"What did you do?" I ask.

"He ran our asses off." David shuffles to his room.

"Are you all right?" I ask. Marie, sad-faced, is at my side. I warn her not to interfere. This is man talk.

"Yeah, yeah. I threw up, that's all."

Later in the season I get the details from David, Andy, and other players. Wind sprints. Calisthenics. Sight-and-sound drills.

Grass drills. Oklahomas. Eye-openers. The hated sled. Fifty-yard-ers. Long-distance runs up and down the hill and around the property. Heat exhaustion, fainting, collapses.

"I don't understand any of this," I say to David. "What's an Oklahoma?"

He averts his head, disgusted by my ignorance. How can I be so thick? It is understandable that I am an ignoramus about hockey. But football? The game I watch with dulled eye and loose jaw for endless hours?

"An Oklahoma is when the coach throws a loose ball and two guys fight for it."

"What's an eye-opener?"

"One kid has the ball, one blocks, one has to fight off the blocker and make the tackle."

"What else?"

"When Mr. Stanley gets sore at us for dogging it, he makes us run the hill. Twice around the school grounds if he's really sore."

"Was it hot today?"

"You kidding?"

I wonder if Dave ever dogs it. But he can't. He's co-captain now with Rag LeBlanc. Dimly I recall coming to practice when he was in eighth or ninth grade and finding him cursing, gasping, as he did penalty laps around the field for some act that had aroused the displeasure of the former coach, Wayne Flood. He seemed to earn a lot of this extra duty. It is not that David is lazy. Quite the contrary. He is the best worker in the family—an avid mower of lawns, hauler of rocks, washer of cars. It is merely that his nose gets out of joint when he is given orders in what he considers a rude or insulting manner.

"Did, you, ah, get any extra wind sprints?" I ask one day when he returns from practice looking drained, pale beneath his dirty tan.

"Me? I lead the calisthenics. I run the sight- and sound-drills. If I don't help Buzz shape those guys up, who will?"

From the safety of my car one steamy day—I am enervated in

my light tennis clothes, and the boys on the field are laden with contact gear—I see Dave clapping his hands to his helmet, his pads, his waist, shouting orders to all seventeen of the King squad. Later they have tackling practice. I hear Buzz screaming at him.

"You want to play or you want to be on the bench?" Buzz is shouting. "Stop tackling with your arms, Green. They call you Mean Joe, you better act like Mean Joe."

Stanley moves Dave aside, lets a ballcarrier come at him, hits him with everything—arms, head, chest, neck. The boy is flattened. He gets up wobbling. "That's how to tackle. Football is hitting, hitting, *hitting*. Listen to me, Green, and you, Levison and Eginton. Don't commit yourself. Get an angle on the guy. Don't stick your arms out. Smash into him with *everything*, so he knows he's been stuck."

The drill continues. Ballcarriers keep coming at the linemen—Sillars, Sweet, Wilson taking turns running the football. Buzz's loud, angry voice shivers the leaves of the old oaks and pines. And then I notice a palpable change. The tacklers *are* hitting harder, coming at the runners with everything, smacking them into the ground with audible thwacks and grunts.

I count seven of Dave's tackles. On the eighth he is furiously slamming the ballcarrier to earth. He and his victim rise slowly, with dirtied dignity, shaky in the September haze and heat. It is awful, beautiful. I am filled with equal measures of joy and guilt.

As I drive away, I hear the unified voices of the tiny squad in varying cadences. I see them flopping to the turf, leaping up, flopping again. Dave and LeBlanc are leading the drill. Buzz has his clipboard out. With his assistant coaches, Chris Kelly and Dave Sample, he is reviewing his personnel. It can't take long. Not with seventeen players.

As I drive off the school grounds, my mind is numbed not only by the ferocity of the practice session, the cruel demands it makes on young bodies, but by the extent to which Stanley can punish David verbally—and command his respect. My son has never taken kindly to authority. A free soul, he has always gotten his back up when teachers, counselors, or parents have been firm with him. He'll work, but not without an argument. And here is Buzz Stanley, shouting in his face, insulting him, shaking him, enforcing his iron will. And the boy loves it. Has he found a putative father in the Buzzer, a symbol of everything I'm not? If he has, I don't really mind.

That evening, Ted, David and I shoot fouls in back of our garage. I'm leaving for the Philippines the next day to work on a book. September is always a hinged month, opening doors, turning us a different way. Our lives are in motion. Nancy will be off to finish at Brandeis. Ted will be a sophomore at Columbia. Marie is about to start a new job in Westchester. And David will be "getting things together defensively" for King.

My fingers tingle. My arms are like whips. My eyes are keen. My foul shooting is perfection. Ted gets seven in a row, David eight. But I can't miss. Suddenly I'm seventeen again, playing with the Brooklyn Jewish Center Juniors. I hit ten in a row. Am I so expert because I'm jealous of Buzz's capture of David's loyalties? Not so. It's just that September is here and we're all moving ahead.

My sons scorn my technique. I use the old two-handed schoolyard set shot—ah, memories of Danny Kaplowitz and Ace Goldstein—and propel the ball in a high arc from eye level. Just a soupçon of backspin.

I'm at twelve in a row. Thirteen. The ball keeps swishing through, fluttering the net, noiseless in its rubberoid perfection.

"How'd you get so good?" Ted asks.

"In my youth, I could shoot baskets. I couldn't run and I couldn't fight, and I wasn't much on defense, but I had the outside shot." Fourteen. Fifteen.

"Two-handed?" David asks. "Who shoots that way?"

"Ah, what you've missed." Sixteen bobbles, then drops in. "You've never heard of Dutch Garfinkel? Or Ossie Schechtman? Or the great City College team that almost beat Stanford in the

Garden in 1939? Davey Paris and Whitey Katz and Bernie Fliegel?"

Their suburban eyes look at me as if I had landed from Venus. No one shoots two-handed any more. Seventeen. Eighteen. I will sink fouls forever.

They are stunned into silence. This from a father who has trouble with the Royal Canadian Air Force exercises!

"Don't choke," David says.

"No way," I realize that I must do this to match David's vigor. The father of a boy who spends hot afternoons bruising himself with Oklahomas and eye-openers can do no less. Twenty-two. Twenty-three.

"A new all-time record for Sawmill Road," I brag. "The old master never misses. Columbia had this little guard, Albie Meyers . . ." I hit twenty-four.

"Didn't you play in the army?" Ted asks.

"Sub on the company team."

"Let your fingers linger on the ball as it is released," I heard Hal Greer say. Twenty-five swishes through.

"I will never miss," I inform them. "I will stand here forever and shoot fouls." The sin of *hubris* undoes me. Twenty-six hits the rear of the rim and rolls off the side.

"The big choke," David says. But he is impressed.

"Let's see you guys do better. Go on, Ted."

Into the night they keep trying, hitting twelve in a row, thirteen. But they can't come close to the old man's record twenty-five. Soon they are bored and switch to one-on-one. The old bull of the herd is safe for a while. In my library is a strange book by Theodore Reik, the old Freudian who went beyond Freud. Primal sin and all that. Reik says that not only did the young ape-man kill his father so that he could possess the mother, but the son then made a smorgasbord of the old man's remains. Maybe. Me, I'll settle for a foul-shooting contest, or a game of HORSE. It's easier on the son's digestion, not to mention the father's.

On this note of triumph I leave for the Philippines. Two days later I'm in a Manila hotel room. Five days later, I'm down with tropic stomach and fevers and am unable to pin down the man with whom I am to collaborate on the book. It's a lost cause. I get sicker. He gets more elusive. My agent tells me to come home, that some projects aren't worth it. Never in my life have I failed to deliver on a book. Now I must return a publisher's advance, fly home out $2,000 in personal expenses.

Ill, frustrated, I find I am coming home five weeks sooner than anticipated and hence will be able to see most of David's games. I'll even get to the opener with Rye. In my despairing state, I view the prospect as a mixed blessing. I sniff loss in the wind, defeats heaped on defeats. Has Buzz cured Dave of arm-tackling? Have they learned the 5-3 zone and the 4-4 stack?

Back in Stamford, I'm devoured by jet-lag. Dozing off at noon, I prowl the house at night, nursing migraine with an ice pack and drugs, attacked by that four-o'clock-in-the-morning despair that limns a future of unpaid bills, bad reviews, losing football games. I thank whatever gods there be for station WNCN—now gone, like so many pleasures—which soothes my burning head with the Grand March from *Norma* at 4:30 A.M.

Game day finds me striding the sidelines at Rye Country Day School. It is a dark gray day, like a Paris morning in November, chilly and damp. There is only a scattering of King parents and students in attendance. Last year's shame, this year's dim prospects, have kept the crowd down. This crowd will not roar, it will murmur. But the cheerleaders, bless their snug maroon panties, have arrived. An act of mercy at the last minute. I study their prancing white legs and shimmering blonde hair. Through a kind of sexual fission, I disintegrate into ten little Humbert Humberts.

Roaring, the King squad, led by David and Paul LeBlanc, storms the field. They do their calisthenics and eye-and-hand drills with snap and vigor, applauding their own excellence. David wears the only white helmet. He has also found a white horsecollar, and there are thick white styrofoam coverings on his forearms. Still, from no angle, in no position, does he look the 191 pounds Stanley claims for him in the program.

Rye, in black and gold, looks big, fast, and mean. Al Hall, their coach, is high on this squad. He isn't bothered by King. He is looking ahead to upset St. Luke's, the fastest gun in town. Every Fairchester League team will be eager to knock off St. Luke's and the legendary Siganos.

"Kids look good," says Murray Levison, Andy's father.

Andy is a senior, a tackle, 210 pounds. He is a handsome, fair-skinned boy, well-spoken and mature. He likes to stick. Even Fat Charlie Griffith will not intimidate him the following week.

"Buzz has worked their butts off," I say. "Dave says they really have a chance."

Murray shakes his head. "No offense. No passing game, no big runner without you-know-who . . ."

He nods toward Bobby Fieber. Bobby has not suited up. He is in civvies, sporting a brimmed hat that suggests the war counselor of the San Juan Killers in the East Bronx. Who can blame him preferring soccer? His father, Norm, is with him. Bob's pretty sister Cathy is one of the cheerleaders. The family is loyal to King, but not as loyal as Coach Stanley would like.

"Hi, there. Jack Rutledge here." A burly, ruddy man shakes my hand. He is the father of "Rut" (6′ 3″, 235 pounds), the other tackle. We wish each other well. Murray, a stockbroker, knows that Mr. Rutledge is the President of Bulova. There is some discussion of the book value of stocks, cash flow. I have no idea what they are talking about.

The stock market is confusing to me, but no more so than David's playbook. I look through it one night during my early morning seance with WNCN, and I am stunned. How can these boys remember so much? David, a C student, is still losing out to irregular French verbs. And did he ever learn the secret of *base five?* But here he is memorizing six different defensive formations, signals, alignments. He can't fake the knowledge. He can't "bull-shit" the answers. He must *know* them. Will he? I tremble for him.

SIGNAL	CALL	SITUATION
1. Shake dice	"Slice"	Stock off-tackle. Stop sweep.
2. Right hand to heart	"Pinch"	Use to shut off middle.
3. Salute right eye	"Storm"	Confuse sweep blocking: give our ends a change.
4. Raised clenched fist	"Gap thunder"	Obvious pass. Perhaps First Down gamble. Good for pressure to strength if pattern develops.
5. Both hands on head	4-3 Basic (rotate to strength)	Look to Coach Kelly.
6. From 15-yard line to goal line	6-5 Goal line	Look to coaches.

I don't understand any of it. Besides, it frightens me. The material on offense is even more terrifying. It begins: *The squad must be sold on the idea that ball control is a way of life. We must believe in it.* It ends with these words, which convince me that Stanley is whistling in the dark with his 130-pound backs. *Our VEER offense is one of patience. It requires testing of the defense to find its weaknesses. Then we will exploit those weaknesses, which will lead us to VICTORY.*

It is the absolute determination of these words that upsets me. Ah, but coaches must believe. Year after year Columbia sends its teams out to lose to Princeton and Dartmouth, and, before the Ivy League was formally organized, to Michigan, Georgia, and Army. (The noble Lou Little kept insisting he wanted to schedule Notre Dame.) And yet it was not all defeat. After all, Columbia upset Stanford in the Rose Bowl in 1934. And they stopped Army's winning streak at twenty-one games with an incredible 21-20 victory against all the odds, all the jibes of the disbelievers. *Winners never quit and quitters never win,* David used to tell me when he was twelve years old and we were an inept father-son doubles team. True enough. But losing all the time gets to be a burden. Maybe we should be allowed to quit now and then? Will the world stop if once or twice we give up?

These musings clutter my sleep-starved head as the game gets under way. I stand, screaming, with Murray Levison and Jack Rutledge, watching our white-uniformed sons. Roy Boe stands a bit apart from us. He betrays no emotions. His son Sam is at safety. Rye has the ball at midfield after the kick-off.

Dave is calling defensive signals. King comes out snappily to its 4-3 defense, with David at middle-linebacker. The front four are Esposito, Levison, Rutledge and LeBlanc. Eginton and Sillars are the outside linebackers. They all like to stick. Rye is using a pro set. I recognize the quarterback. He is a red-faced, frizzy-headed boy named Robinson, an excellent passer and runner, a natural athlete. He has been playing against King since sixth grade. Didn't I once see Rye lose to David's lower-grade team, when Pete Fisher was running quarterback sneaks the length of the field?

There is a crash, a collision of bodies. The game scares me. It is like a series of planned disasters. The ball is snapped, bodies hit, churn, fall; someone will gain, someone will lose, someone will be humiliated.

"Good hit, Dave," I hear Murray shouting.

David has made the first tackle of the season. He reads a sweep, refuses to be faked or blocked, runs close to the muddy turf, hits Guarnaccia, Rye's speedy back, with a sure tackle.

Robinson drops back to pass. The pass is high and true, between the linebackers and the defensive backs. David has been pulled out of position. He was fooled on the fake, froze, lost his man. Rye's receiver drops the ball. We applaud.

Hints of doom. Robinson and Guarnaccia probe the line. No good. The center holds. But the ends are vulnerable. Passes are almost always caught. The King secondary seems to be lost in a misty fog. They leave receivers uncovered, fall down, falter, make wrong turns. The game is two minutes old and they score on a pass into the end zone. The receiver walks in untouched.

Rye kicks off. Cameron Sillars makes a respectable return. I like him. He moves awkwardly in stiff-legged strides. King goes into its V-set. Now, for the first time anywhere, Buzz Stanley's "veer" offense. I'm still not sure I understand it. But it works. It works.

Jimmy Wilson, frail and young, gets over the center, LeBlanc. He hands to Sillars. Dave blows his man out. Eight yards off tackle. Chris Sweet, the 212-pound freshman fullback, runs for four, then five more. The offensive blocking is crisp and accurate. Andy Levison, Eginton, Dave, LeBlanc, Rutledge are moving the black jerseys. *A first down!* Wilson runs along the line of scrimmage, tosses to Sillars, and Cam, following his blocking, goes for ten yards and another first down. ("That's Oklahoma football at its best," Buzz will tell me later when we look at the films.)

"These kids can do it," Murray says. "They've got it together."

Wilson keeps and picks up four yards. John Eginton is offside.

Wilson tries a pass, slips before he can get the ball off. ("We now went into our extremely limited passing game," Buzz explains the next day.) Sam Boe punts. Rye's ball at midfield. Suddenly the disaster I have been fearing since the kick-off strikes. Rye goes wide into a double wing. Robinson fakes, turns the right end and runs fifty yards for a touchdown. He seems to be laughing as he races past the King defenders. The linebackers and defensive backs fail to "play their lanes." I look for David; he is lost. Rye makes the extra points on another sweep. It's 14-0.

Football is so terribly unfair. Like life. Like art. Like book reviewing. The King team looked so splendid for four minutes. And with a single bootleg run, the game is falling away. Wilson tries another pass. It's intercepted. (He throws bravely on the run, throws soft passes off the flat of his hand. Years ago Columbia had a back who threw the same odd passes, a certain Jumping Jack Naylor. And a losing team.)

"Come up and pop," I hear one of the King coaches yelling.

"Stick," another exhorts them.

But the Rye coach knows something. He can sweep the ends.

They drive deep. Robinson fakes, fools the King linebackers, throws a pass for a touchdown.

"Dave covered the wrong man," I say apologetically to Murray Levison.

"Hell, they were all nowhere. No pass rush. Andy was dead on his feet."

David stops the extra point with a hard tackle. He's still hitting. Dick Whitcomb, St. Luke's coach, drifts by. He looks happy. He will play King next week, Rye in a few weeks. I am tempted to ask him for mercy. If Rye is doing this to King, what will St. Luke's do to my son and his teammates?

"See anything?" I ask Whitcomb.

He smiles. "Two teams. I'll never know why Buzz scheduled us."

"To keep the league intact."

He shrugs. "Long season for those kids. They're all being scouted today. There's Jim Bean of Hamden Hall and Dick Conti of Deaf."

Being scouted. Will I survive seven more games?

Sillars fumbles. Rye recovers. Guarnaccia is popped by Dave on an off-tackle play and coughs the ball up. The fathers let out a yell. *All is not lost!* Down 20-0 is like being tied. I watch Dave as he sticks the runner—measures him, waits, gets low, crashes, into him with everything. ("Best stick of the game," Buzz says the following day. "We were hot and cold. They couldn't run the middle, but they killed us with sweeps and passes.")

Bobby Fieber, the nonplaying runner, comes by. He looks pained. I don't know why he's here. He says: "I get a dirty look from Buzz every time I walk past the bench." I feel sorry for Bobby but worse for King. Rye has just scored again on a sweep of right end. And two extra points on the identical sweep. It's 28-0 at the half.

Yet in some nutty way, King doesn't look that bad. They just seem hesitant, afraid to hit, unaware of their potential. But as the second half begins, they move well. On offense, Jimmy Wilson reads the defenders, keeps, runs twelve yards. Sillars picks up yardage with his stiff-legged lope. Dave trades a few punches with a Rye tackle. They stop quickly. No penalty. ("I know the game is lost," Buzz says to me the next day, "but I can't tell the kids. All we worked for is down the drain in the first game, against a not very good team.")

Fourteen-year-old Chris Sweet is dragging five Rye tacklers for a six-yard gain. A gentle, pink-faced boy, appropriately named, he did not want to play football. Buzz worked on him all summer. He has never played a game until today. Wilson fumbles. Sillars tries to recover. Someone steps on his face. Robinson throws another bomb. The receiver runs away from the defensive backs and it's 34-0. The extra points—yes, a sweep—make it 36-0.

I can't wait for the clock to end the torment. I decide that I hate football. Now I know why Marie won't attend the games. David is covered with dirt, sweating, his face black. He seems to be cursing at his own defensive linemen every time they go into huddle. Buzz is shouting for downfield blocking. No one is picking up on tacklers. No one wants to stick except a few hard-heads like Dave, Andy, Eginton, Sillars.

King keeps missing first downs by a foot, losing the ball on fumbles. Good drives are stopped by penalties. Wilson throws eleven yards to Ralph Esposito. No one has told Espo they are down 36-0. He battles for a few more yards with seven Rye players hanging on to him. Dave leads a wedge of blocking for Sillars. Rye tackles Sillars, but there's a face-mask penalty.

"Christ, we're blowing their defensive line out three yards every shot," I hear Buzz say to Kelly. "How in hell are we down 36-0?"

Rye's ball. David sticks Guarnaccia again. Trying to salvage some honor, he tells me later that he taunted the runner: "I stuck your ass, kid." And what was the reply, I ask. "Up yours, 51."

Fair enough. Rye deserves the game. But why does Stanley keep stopping the clock by calling time or throwing out of bounds? He is intent on a score. King is driving in the fourth quarter. ("The most humiliating day of my life up to then," Buzz says the next day. "Until St. Luke's.") I want to run the clock, keep it going, end the agony. David can barely drag himself to his feet. He has run over five hundred yards, he tells me after the game. His feet hurt. He has a charley horse.

Late in the game I see David wobbling. He takes his helmet off during time-out, rubs his forehead. Is he hurt? Buzz is yelling at him to look at him for a defensive formation. He wants a five-man line. David does not acknowledge him. He walks in circles, holding his head. I pray he is not injured. (Buzz delights in telling the boys about injuries. His rule for avoiding them is simple: *Hit the other guy first and hit him harder.*)

Stanley is on the field, holding fingers in front of David's face. Contemptuously, David puts his helmet back on and ties the chin strap. He spits. Buzz again holds fingers up for him to see. They seem to be laughing.

I eavesdrop as Buzz runs off the field. "Green's okay. Just shaken up. I asked him how many fingers, and he said 'two' and I got sore at him. He knew I had five. He's all right."

This is a part of the game I will not describe to Marie.

"Tough game for your kid," Dick Whitcomb says.

"For all of them."

"Buzz has a rebuilding job. It's hard when a school gives the game up for a year."

"Dick, why not play your jayvees against them?" I ask. "I mean, give the kids a break. Siganos and all . . ."

Whitcomb chuckles. "Ready for a funny story about Siganos?"

"Anything." King has fumbled again. Rye runs a play. Buzz calls a time-out. He wants the ball. He wants a score.

"Siganos is five-nine, and he stuffs," Whitcomb says. "That's right. He can leap off a basketball floor, get over the rim, and stuff it down."

Levison, Rutledge, Fieber, and I listen like the parents of young Christians getting a rundown from the lion-keeper. "The word got out, and these coaches all over the south are calling me to find out if Siganos is . . . well . . . *colored.* They can't believe a white man five-nine can stuff a basketball. They always begin, "That there boy Siganos y'all got, is he a nigger? If'n he's a nigger, we ain't interested, but if'n he's white . . . that's different.' "

We laugh politely.

Whitcomb goes on. "They say they don't mind local blacks who know their place, but they won't recruit blacks from up North. Couple of 'em wanted Mike's photo to make sure he was white."

"Where's he going?" Murray asks.

"Probably Kentucky. They believed me right off. Just wanted his stats."

As we talk Robinson strolls into the end zone, and the score is 42-0, where it will stay until the merciful whistle blows. In the fading moments, someone on King fumbles again. Wilson? Sillars? I have lost track.

The King team drags itself toward the sidelines. They have brought football back and to what end? I approach hesitantly, with Murray Levison, Jack Rutledge, Warren Eginton, a few other parents.

David's face is caked with mud. There is a bloody ridge along his forehead. He is raging. His Neapolitan eyes are on fire. His mouth is tight. He looks as if he wants to hit everyone in sight, I am afraid to go near him, but I do.

"It's all right, Dave," I said. "You guys will get better. They beat you outside."

"That's right." Murray says. "They didn't get a yard up the middle. You did your job."

"And you blew them out on offense," Warren Eginton adds.

We are greeted by solemn, angry, pained glares.

"We stunk," David says. His voice is quivering with fury. "We stunk."

Buzz, red-faced, chest heaving, walks out with his beaten charges. "Okay, put it behind you," I hear him say. "You people will have to learn to stick. You will have to come up and pop people. We're going to find players who aren't afraid to stick."

Where? I wonder. With twenty men suited up and only a baker's dozen who are capable of playing the game?

I hear David's rage-clotted voice once more as they walk off, dirtied and defeated. "We stunk."

"Couldn't say it better myself," Murray Levison says to me. We don't smile. We are miserable middle-aged men and we can do nothing for our sons.

5

"Vince would have made a great President," Buzz says. He is moody, gloomy. We've just watched the films of the St. Luke's game. King's opponents have scored 104 points in two games. King has scored 6.

I don't know how the subject has gotten to be politics. The boys yawn, stretch. They are battered and frustrated. Someone had made a crack about Nixon, and Buzz had jumped on him. "He's better than anyone else around," the coach says. "He's got his faults, but who hasn't?"

Liberal that I am, old New Dealer, raised with heroes like Herbert H. Lehman and Harold Ickes, I hold my tongue. The boys say nothing. For all I know, most of them come from homes where Nixon is given the benefit of the doubt. It's Fairfield County, after all—Darien, New Canaan, Greenwich. In Stamford at least we have slums, blacks, factories, a handful of political activists.

"Vince?" I ask. No, I am not a real American. My interest in football, in Dave's embattled career, is a fraud. I know *which* Vince. I just won't admit it.

"Lombardi," Buzz says. He packs up the projector. The last play is imprinted on my brain, Xeroxed onto the gray cells. Steve Smith crushing David to earth, stepping on his crotch, spine, jaw, leaving him with fractured speech and a ringing skull.

74

"Yeah," the coach goes on. "Winning is the *only* thing. You guys are going to learn it. We'll find people who like to hit. Put St. Luke's behind you."

President Lombardi. What can I say? How can I establish my credentials as something other than what I am? I, who never *stuck?* My years as a newsman help. I can conjure up odd stories, strange tales, interesting in themselves but noncommittal. I can hide my suspect liberalism behind trivia. "Funny thing," I say. "I worked a political convention for NBC one year. Bear Bryant got two votes from the Alabama delegation."

"For President?" asks Buzz.

"Yes. The Democratic nomination."

"He'd have made one hell of a President. That's what the country needs. Leadership. Discipline." Bear is the culture hero of all Southern coaches. Buzz's years at Wake Forest have conditioned him. Bear Bryant is a father figure, a paragon, a way of life.

Levison, Sillars, Rutledge, Wilson, LeBlanc, and the others mumble, tease, display the nervousness of adolescence. They aren't sure if Buzz and I are joking.

The subject changes abruptly. "God, I hate this Thursday game," the coach says. "These kids will still be hurting, banged up by St. Luke's. Everything's going against you people, you know that, don't you?"

The opponent is the New York School for the Deaf. They've never been a power. I remember David playing on lower-school teams that beat them regularly.

"They get all the breaks," Buzz says, "so you people better be alert. They can play nineteen-year-olds. Half the team is nineteen, maybe older. They don't call signals. They move on a cadence. And I'm warning you, the refs favor them."

Andy Levison speaks up. "You said we could beat them anyway, Coach."

"Damn right. This is our first win."

I stare at the signs around the office. DON'T COUNT THE DAYS, MAKE THE DAYS COUNT. THE DAY OF THE GAME

IS THE DAY TO MAKE GOOD; THE DAY AFTER IS TOO LATE.

If strength, speed, athletic skills could be absorbed through sheer contact with the written word, Buzz's boys would be tigers. No matter which way they turn their heads, they are greeted by neatly lettered advice pointing the road to victory. IT'S NOT THE SIZE OF THE BOY IN THE FIGHT, IT'S THE SIZE OF THE FIGHT IN THE BOY.

Someone brings the conversation back to current events. The Yom Kippur War has broken out.

Buzz yawns widely. "I pick the Israelis in the fourth quarter," he says.

The Deaf game is almost too painful to recall. It was not only a loss—and to a team they were convinced they would beat—it was a personal humiliation for David. I could hear him on the phone, locked in his room after the disaster, reviewing the tragedy with Levison, consoling Sillars, appealing to Feiber to come out for the team. (Bobby had asked Buzz if he could kick against NYSD but not run. "You play for me, you play all the way," Stanley had told him firmly.)

A clear, bright, glorious October day. A field in White Plains, New York. The Deaf kids are in blue and gray. King looks snappy and psyched up in its clean white uniforms. I marvel that after two crushing defeats they can be this eager, in such good shape.

"Buzz says they've scouted us twice," Murray Levison tells me as we await the kick-off.

"Then they'll lose. Overconfidence."

"He hasn't scouted them but he saw some old films. The coach, Dick Conti, is an old buddy of Buzz's." We look at the Deaf players. They look enormous. Against Mike Mori at 101? And Sillars and Wilson, at about 135 each?

"That's their star," Murray says. "If they stop him, they can do it."

Levison indicates a tall, broad-shouldered black boy, number

42. "Odom. He's six-two and a hundred and ninety pounds. West-chester County two-twenty yard champ. He's the offense. Once he sweeps, forget it."

"We haven't any Odom."

"Sweet and Sillars looked good against Rye. You know we al-most out-statisticked them?"

An argument is going on before the game starts. Buzz doesn't like the fact that both benches are on the same side of the field. It makes one sideline dangerous. And the field is dangerous enough, surrounded as it is by a macadam track. He loses. The benches stay. But he has not endeared himself to the officials. I recognize some of the other league coaches. It's a Thursday and they all have a chance to look King and Deaf over. There's Jim Bean of Hamden Hall, Al Hall of Rye—they play a second game against King next week—and someone from the mysterious new entry on the schedule, St. Hugh's of New York City.

"Buzz has a few surprises," Murray tells me. Jack Rutledge joins us. "He's using Boe as a wide receiver. But he also moves over in a quarterback-in-motion series. He's their best passer."

I remember Sam Boe getting crushed to earth, vanishing under St. Luke's players. And Andy's description: "The poor guy didn't know if he should laugh or cry." (Buzz describes it differently: *He came of age.*)

King gets the kick-off. Immediately the blocking is crisp, pun-ishing. Dave and Andy and Rut and Eginton and LeBlanc are shoving the defensive line back. They hit hard, blow defenders into the linebackers. Sweet hits for four, Sillars for eleven.

"Amazing how good these kids can look," I say to Levison.

Big Rutledge is offside. The next two running plays are stopped. A Wilson pass is short.

"And how bad," Murray says. "But they can play this team."

The punt is poor. Deaf has the ball on its own twenty. They come out in a double wing. There is no cadence. They move on the snap of the ball. King's defense is utterly unprepared, sur-prised by the strange procedure. Odom races outside. Cameron

Sillars is sucked in. Untouched, Odom races into the end zone. The game is a minute and eleven seconds old and King is behind 6-0.

Dumbfounded, King lines up to defend against the extra point. They expect Odom wide again. He plunges up the middle. The score is now 8-0 with a minute and eleven gone.

"Another Rye?" I ask Jack Rutledge.

"I hope not. Those poor kids."

I think of Rutledge and Levison discussing book values, bond issues, earning ratios, and I feel alien to them. Perhaps I should not even be here watching the tormenting of our children. My wife has the right idea. She is home boning up for her master's degree. After bloody St. Luke's, nothing will get her to watch King play.

"Mrs. Eginton comes to all the games," I argue. "Mrs. Rutledge does."

"That's their privilege. I hate it. And I don't like the way you glory in watching him get murdered every weekend."

And then King is moving beautifully again. The front line, with David and Eginton leading the blocking, is shoving Deaf all over the field. Sillars for four. Wilson keeping for twelve. Sweet for five. They're on Deaf's forty-two-yard line. They can run all day. Sillars fumbles, Deaf recovers.

As Deaf lines up, we hear Buzz screaming at the referee. "Ref! They're *encroaching* on the ball! They're lining up offside!" He's waving at the blue-gray of Deaf athletes. "Their line is playing with heads past the ball! They're not leaving a lane!"

He is still screaming as Odom races past the secondary, catches a pass, and runs forty-two yards for another touchdown.

Murray, Rutledge, Eginton, and I are silent. Our eyes are dim. Our jaws are tight. We are still silent as Odom runs outside for the extra point. The game is four minutes old and King is down 16-0.

Only Roy Boe, Sam's father, looks unruffled. He keeps his distance. A handsome, self-disciplined man. I envy him. Later in the season he will endow King School with a whirlpool bath and a universal gym. ("A quarterback and a few runners would have helped," Murray Levison says to me on learning of Mr. Boe's largesse.)

The rest of the quarter is desultory. The teams try a few plays, kick, hold. Buzz is still yelling about Deaf's encroaching on the ball. Toward the end of the first quarter I see Assistant Coach Dave Sample taking Polaroid photos of the line of scrimmage. It does no good. During a time-out, Buzz waves them at the referee. "They're consistently over the ball on offense and defense," he shouts. "I have the proof. Our kids are getting hit before the snap."

"Get back there and shut up or I'll have you thrown out," the referee responds.

Buzz's huge face is scarlet. "That guy's known me for years. He's got it in for me."

Second quarter. Stanley's "veer" offense is a thing of beauty. I marvel at the precision. He is a superb coach. The plays are executed with snap, direction, deception. It is inconceivable that the team can be losing 16-0. Sillars, Wilson, and Sweet take turns carrying. Wilson gets off a perfect fifteen-yard pass to Boe. They have moved from their own sixteen-yard line to Deaf's four. They are dominating the game. In spite of Deaf's "encroachment," they are blasting them back, opening wide holes in Deaf's heavy line.

It is now fourth down and a foot to go for a first down on Deaf's four-yard line. The play is sent in from the bench: a 26 slant off-tackle, with Green leading the blocking. He must move his man. There's the snap. Sillars takes the handoff from Wilson. David obliterates his man. Sillars races in standing up. We are screaming, cheering. My eyes are wet. "Stick 'em Dave," I yell. It's better than a good notice in *Publishers Weekly*.

Are we cursed? The play is called back. Offside. On King. Who? It's David. Buzz is shrieking at him. "Dope! What the hell is wrong with you?"

I avert my eyes. Reversing the Biblical story, I cannot look upon

my son in his nakedness. The shame is all his. *Offside*. David. Who
led the blocking. The words choke in my throat. My brain is mud-
died with memories of my own lost games, double faults, missed
grounders.

Fourth down, five yards to go. Sillars tries again. He's short.
Deaf takes over.

It is the nadir of the season for me, for David. Nothing can get
worse. I am almost buoyed by this appalling knowledge. Suddenly
everything seems to come loose for King. Deaf punts. A personal
foul is called against John Eginton—fifteen yards lost. As soon as
King lines up, deep in its own territory, the ref blows his whistle. We look on, stunned. We are being penalized another fifteen
yards.

"What's up?" Buzz shouts.

The referee comes to the sidelines. "Your quarterback had his
chinstrap loose," he says. "That's fifteen yards."

Buzz claps his hands to his head. "That's a New York rule and
it's never enforced. We play Connecticut rules. The chinstrap can
be loose. You guys are out to kill us."

Deep in my black heart, I am almost happy that John Eginton
and Jimmy Wilson are at fault. It draws attention away from
David's dreadful lapse. No. His was worse. *Offside on a touchdown*. It could have been 16-6 now. Maybe 16-8. They were
shoving Deaf all over the field. How can such a good line, such a
good running attack, be so bad?

"What about them encroaching?" Buzz yells. "You don't call
that. You're a bunch of homers."

The ref glares at him. "If you don't shut your bazoo, Stanley,
you can get on the bus."

"Listen," Stanley pleads. "You can't tell how offside they are
from the end zone. For Chrissake, watch a play from the sidelines and you'll see they're offside almost every time they line up."

"Once more, Stanley. The bus."

Another penalty is called for a loose chinstrap. I'm afraid to say
anything but I have the feeling that Buzz is right. He's reached

the point of no return with the officials. Maybe they are "homers," maybe not. But they seem to have made their minds up that King cannot win. (In a secret compartment of my mind, I assure myself that David was *not* offside on the four-yard line. It was a bum call, a blatant move to nullify the touchdown run.)

"Look at that," I hear Dave Sample say. "When a Deaf kid has his strap loose, the official taps him on the arm and points to it. 'Tie it, kid, watch it.' Our kids get the penalty."

As the end of the half approaches, King is moving again, short, hard runs. Like an old Jock Sutherland team at Pittsburgh. They are grinding out yardage, shoving the Deaf defenders into the turf. They are deep in Deaf territory when someone else is called for a loose chinstrap. At the half, Deaf leads 16–0. A record has gotten stuck in my head. It keeps repeating: *Dave was offside, Dave was offside.* I try to pick up the needle and move it on but I can't. None of the other fathers mentions it to me. I watch the team, frustrated, furious, move to the locker room, and I wonder what lunacy has made me get involved in my son's football. Cobbler, stick to thy last. Physician, heal thyself. Writer, stay with your damned typewriter and don't try to match muscles with jocks.

There's always a second half. What I tend to ignore, as I chat with the other fathers, is that there's a second half for our opponents too. But we've unquestionably dominated them.

"The kids are getting there," says Murray Levison.

Warren Eginton adds: "They look better. They'll get it together."

But will they? We kick off. There's inept coverage, and Deaf has the ball at midfield. On the first play they reverse Odom, and he runs fifty-seven yards for a touchdown. David is nowhere. Edge misses a tackle. It's 22–0. The extra point is stopped.

Then, oddly, on the next series of plays, I notice that David is on the sidelines. Chris Kelly is raging at him. "You failed to box in. You stink. Odom ran around you. What kind of linebacker are you?"

Shame, fear, rage wash over me. (I am nonsensically reminded of a book in my father's medical library: *Bodily Changes in Fear, Pain, Hunger and Rage*. I even recall the author's name: Walter B. Cannon.)

David is pleading. "Let me back in. I made seven tackles. We're hurting those guys."

"You stay here until you learn to box in."

King's on offense. A sophomore goes in for David. Deep in my heart I'm glad he's getting a rest. Normally he plays the entire game, offense and defense.

The coaches seem to have lost control of the game. Isaacs, a 130-pound cornerback, is pulled out. "You did a lousy job," Buzz Stanley shouts at him. "You didn't support."

Isaacs is howling, holding his nose. "Support! Jesus, look at my nose!" Isaacs's nose is red and swollen. Later they learn it's broken. He'll be lost for five games.

David's short fuse is sputtering. He stalks Kelly on the sidelines. "I didn't deserve to be taken out," he says.

"Then get back in and play football."

"Dammit, they're still encroaching," Buzz cries to an unhearing world. "Our guys have to beat the ref *and* the team." He refuses to flinch under an angry glare from the official. To his assistants he mutters: "Guy knows me from way back. He threw me out of a basketball game last year."

Curious how King can, for stretches, move the ball with the beautiful precision of the "veer." The Deaf team is staggering, dragging itself to the line. Three of them will be out of next week's game. King is on their twenty when Sillars fumbles. On the next play, Andy Levison hits the Deaf quarterback, who obliges by fumbling the ball back.

We can do it. Nothing is impossible. Two plays later, behind picture-book blocking, Sillars lopes in for a touchdown. Dave, Edge, Andy, Rut, and LeBlanc obliterate the Deaf defenders. The extra point is short. But it's still a ball game at 22-6.

"You guys can win it!" Buzz shouts.

Again and again, Odom is stopped. He's had his moments of glory. It's going to be King's game. We sense it. The ground game is chewing muddy chunks of yardage out of the field. Halfway through the third quarter, they're on Deaf's six-yard line. It's fourth down and a yard, almost the identical situation as in first-quarter play when Dave was offside.

This time there will be no mistake. They will get the yard. They will get the touchdown. They will win. We sense it.

Buzz calls time-out. He wants a "Power I 36 drive." The second back through the hole that Dave will open, Sillars, will carry for the first down or the touchdown.

The coach tells Jimmy Wilson: "If you see them shift, call a 'Gold' automatic and take the ball yourself. Goose LeBlanc to give him the signal and go up the middle if the linebacker moves outside. You got it?"

We watch nervously. I am afflicted again with my Columbia-bred sense of disaster.

The Deaf middle linebacker moves left. There's an open space ahead of the center. Jimmy Wilson gooses LeBlanc and calls the "Gold" automatic. He'll carry it himself. He rises ever so slightly on his toes.

Before the play can be run, the referee's whistle is shrieking. It is beyond our comprehension. Buzz is racing down the sideline. "What goes?" he shouts. "What happened?"

The ref gives the signal: *backfield in motion.* He is claiming that Wilson moved. King is being set back five yards. "He didn't move!" Buzz pleads. "He didn't move!"

Wilson is appealing to the official. Later, Jim Bean, the Hamden Hall coach, watching from beyond the end zone, tells Buzz: "The kid never moved. It was a horseshit call. You were jobbed."

Twice more King drives to the Deaf goal. Once Wilson fumbles on the thirty-yard line. The second time Sillars runs twenty-five yards and is called back because his chinstrap is loose. The game ends.

On a silent bus, Buzz tells the team: "You were robbed. That was your game. That was the worst house job I ever saw in my life. Don't be downhearted. The refs stole the game from you."

David tells me all this at a dinner table that has the atmosphere of a mourners' bench. He only half believes it. He had a bad game. He was offside on a touchdown. He did not box in. He did not support. Kelly benched him for part of the third quarter. If the team played poorly, he, captain and defensive leader, was one of the poorest.

"I stunk," he says. He rises from the table, his pork chops untouched.

"You had a bad game," I say. "Forget it. There's always next week." (Next week is Rye, which has already beaten them 42-0.)

"I stunk."

His misery, so complete and so resistant to fake comforts, stabs at my innards. Last week, after the drubbing by St. Luke's, he had a bruised jaw, but he had his pride. To the very last he was sticking. This week he has a ravaged heart. Nothing helps.

"You take it too seriously," Marie says, after he has left. "That's why he takes it so hard."

"Not at all. It's how he plays the game. The boy wants to win."

Exhausted, David collapses on his bed. The postgame party—usually at Rutledge's home in Darien—is forgone this time. I offer no more phony comforts and consolations. He's beyond that. He will hate himself for a day or two. But he will not quit. He will not let Buzz down. He will not let football die at King School.

I tread moodily past his room, catching the laminated stench of dog, sweatsocks, jocks, old leather. Hockey equipment fills a quarter of the floor space. Ski boots rest on top of fishing tackle. Tennis rackets lie athwart cleats.

In the corridor Marie has hung family photos. There's one of the Greens at Westhampton Beach in 1957. David is a year and a half old. His head looks the size of a peach. His neck can be circled with a loose-leaf ring. He is frail, pot-bellied, bandy-legged. His bathing trunks droop below the baby paunch. Then I recall: he could not drink milk. Allergic reaction. We finally learned to feed him Mull-Soy, a soy-bean extract. Remembering the change it produced in him, I marvel. The neck thickened, the belly flattened, the shoulders broadened. The legs grew into thick muscular columns. Years later I met the son of Dr. Muller, who invented Mull-Soy. I thanked him for his father's nutritive help to David. The milk substitute did its work, transformed him from a wobbly weakling to a pulling guard.

If only, I muse, it had helped his temperament. A little less anger, tenseness, hatred of losing. No, that's wrong too. It's what makes him love to *stick*. Vaguely, I think of suggesting a Mull-Soy regimen for the team. Would it stop fumbles? Offsides? Prejudiced officials?

Through the door, I hear David on the phone talking to Andy. "Three of their guys are out. We really blew them out. They were hurting when it was over. What? Sure we have a chance against Rye."

All is not lost.

6

At some point during the season, the Romanesque Cathedral of Bitonto gets intertwined with King football.

It's a long-term project for art history. Mrs. Eastman gives the assignment: a scale model, in whatever medium the student wishes to use, of either a Romanesque or a Renaissance Italian cathedral.

It seems to me an appallingly ambitious burden for a seventeen-year-old who has to learn a completely new defense. Buzz has some surprises in store for Rye. They won't sweep his ends again. He's holding secret practices, letting the word out that his kids are down, afraid to play Rye a second time. In the middle of all this intense concentration, David has to consider a cathedral.

"What is he doing taking art history, anyway?" I demand of Marie. I'm afraid to ask him anything since the Deaf disaster. He blames himself for the loss.

"Senior year. Gut courses. Look at his program. *Theory of comedy. Minorities in the New World. Art history. French IV.*"

"Good God, whatever happened to calculus and American history?"

"He's completed all his requirements."

"*French?* He's been taking French since fourth grade when we lived in Paris, and he's still getting C's."

"I spoke to his teacher. His accent is perfect, but grammar doesn't interest him."

"It would if they had offensive and defensive grammar."

The building of the cathedral unnerves him. He wants an easy one, something that won't interfere with the new 6-2 Gap Thunder or the new series of "veer" plays off the I formation.

Ever since we lived in Italy, in 1959 and 1960, I have been an Italophile. In the sweet, restful future when there are no more losing football seasons, I will live in Florence and write a book about Italy. Any kind of book. I want to set it down before it all disappears, the Perugino blue skies, the crumbling baroque façades, the cool churches, the secret museums. I find a book on Italian architecture full of simple line drawings and give it to David. "Pick a cathedral," I say. "I'll help you start it."

He's at his desk. Ah, homework. No, it's Buzz's "Offensive Checklist." I read some of it.

FULL HOUSE
QB sneak
24 dive
26 slant
28 power
29 pitch
36 dive
19 power
11 power
41 pitch

The subject switches from Norman Romanesque to full house backfields.

"Explain this," I say. "These are plays that come off a full house backfield? Three backs lined up behind the quarterback?"

"That's right."

"And you have a different assignment each time?"

"Not always. I just have to blow a guy out."

"I see. And how many formations do you run out of?"

"Five main formations. Full house, wishbone, V set, power I,

I set. Then we also have the direct-snap series with Boe passing or the Esposito special, the end-around pass."

"And how many plays from each formation? Just the main five?"

"About ten. About fifty different plays, but Buzz says we can run a total of 189 different plays."

"And you have to know them all? And a new defense this week?"

"That's right. Dad, will you please let me study?"

Study? I wonder how he will ever absorb all this information. And to what end? To be drubbed, charley-horsed, and suffer the misery of losing games? Still, it's his life. And I seem to enjoy it.

Marie and I wish, though, that he'd apply that prodigious capacity for memorizing "24 traps" and "26 scissors" to his courses. But perhaps he's better off as a steady C student. We mull his options, decide that as long as he passes courses, he needn't worry about competing with his straight A sister at Brandeis and his A-minus brother at Columbia. These musings lead me to Green's Law.

"It's crazy," I say to Marie. "David's friends, most of them jocks, are strictly the C-minus club. But have you noticed that their families all have forty-foot in-ground pools designed by Wagner? Ted's friends are B students, and the families own above-ground vinyl-liner jobs. Fair enough. Nancy's crowd were all A students, National Merit scholars, so brilliant you wanted to strangle them, and *there wasn't a pool in the group*. What does it prove?"

"I'm not sure."

"It's Green's Law. The higher the intellectual attainment of the child, the less the likelihood of a large pool. The lower the IQ, College Boards, class ranks, the greater that likelihood. It tells us a great deal about values in the effete East, but I don't think I want to look into it too deeply."

Late at night I hear David in the cellar. He is sawing old plywood left over from a go-cart he built when he was eleven into an approximation of the façade of the Cathedral of Bitonto. He has made some erratic tracings on tissue paper and transferred them to the plywood.

"Not bad," I say. "Leave enough room at the top for the rose window. And if I may make a suggestion, don't try to do the detail work on the wooden surface. You can paste smooth cardboard on to it, and work in the carvings and windows with Magic Markers."

"Yeah, yeah."

He keeps sawing. I feel guilty, letting art history take him away from his "34 counters" and "26 dive isolates." Yet as I leave the dim cellar, with a soft October rain pecking at the windows, I am full of hope. Life is rich with drama, color, wonders. A twelfth-century cathedral in the Apulia. A perfectly executed 21 quick pitch off a wishbone slant. He's got a little of both worlds, and I'm reasonably happy for him.

Big excitement: Bobby Fieber will start in the second Rye game. Buzz Stanley has worked his rough magic on him. Buzz was firm. He spurned Fieber's offer to do the kicking only. You run for me or you don't play, the coach says. So Bobby will start at fullback, taking fourteen-year-old Chris Sweet's place next to Cam Sillars. It will surely make a difference in the ground game. But a 42-point difference?

"I went against all I've ever believed in, letting that kid come out for the team after refusing to play in three games," Buzz tells me. "But I needed him."

Coach Stanley reminds me of the late Harry Cohn, the head of Columbia Pictures. During the McCarthy era, Los Angeles patriots warned him that it would be unwise to hire Communists or Red sympathizers. In his vast office, flanked by dozens of Oscars, Cohn all but saluted as he responded in a clear voice: "I will never hire a Communist, unless I need him." The assorted Legionnaires, watchdogs, and aroused mothers left satisfied. But I don't tell the story to Buzz. It might muddle our relationship.

Fieber's appearance stimulates a few more no-shows to come

out. John Daum, the soccer goalie, the best pass receiver at King, turns up for football practice. Daum has an old head injury, and he's understandably concerned. Buzz has a special helmet made for him. "Paid for it out of my own pocket," he says. Daum will give them a pair of good hands, Fieber a vastly improved running game.

But it is the defense that Stanley is counting on to turn the tables on Rye. I'm stunned. After a 42-0 shellacking?

"Look at the statistics. They gained nine yards through the middle of our line and a hundred and fifty-nine yards on sweeps." Buzz tells Assistant Coaches Dave Sample and Chris Kelly, "If I were Al Hall, I'd run the hell out of our ends again. He knows we used the same defense against St. Luke's and Deaf. Let's go with something new."

The something new is sheer brilliance. It convinces me that Buzz Stanley, given the material, would be the best coach in the league. In secret practice sessions, Buzz teaches his young team the *Wide Tackle Six*.

"Basically, it's a six-man front, with the defensive ends really linebackers moved forward. They don't get into a three point, they stand up. The middle four are down. We gap the guards to the outside. That's why we call it *wide tackle*."

The new defensive alignment is completely different:

LE-Green	LT-LeBlanc	LG-Hart	RG-Rutledge	RT-Levison	RE-Eginton
	LLB-Sillars			RLB-Wilson	
DB-Mori		S-Boe			DB-Barrett

I note the crucial changes. Dave and John Eginton, linebackers, are on the line of scrimmage. Injuries to other starters have moved tiny Mike Mori (Little Wimp) into a defensive back position, along with Mark Barrett, at about 135 pounds. The two linebackers, Wilson and Sillars, are also undersized, but they are fearless, hard-hitting kids. It looks interesting. But will it work?

"I want this game bad," Buzz says to me. "Al Hall, the Rye

coach, is an old friend. I respect him and he respects me. It's important for me to win after the way they humiliated us. I know we were young and scared but they weren't forty-two points better. The stats prove it."

It's sunny and clear again at King School. The first home game! I look at the rickety stands, the lush green field, the barn-red buildings, the old shade trees. It's a lovely place. David has had good years here, even though he joins in the requisite senior criticism of the school. "It's ridiculous," he tells me. "A senior class with twenty-nine kids. It doesn't make sense!" Someday he will learn the value of small groups. We sent him to King because he was having difficulties in public school. A slow reader, an enemy of homework. I knew what the problem was. He had been going to school since he was two. By the time he got to first grade the notion was implanted in him that school was for horsing around. You went on "sliding pines" and made colored cut-outs. Studying and learning were not part of his scheme of things at age six.

I'm grateful to King. It taught David to read—with assists from a voluminous library of paperbound sports books. It taught him he had to study, occasionally. And it gave him an outlet for his energy and his strength. I smile at John Vance, the headmaster. We agree it would be nice if King made the home opener a winner.

"What's Stanley up to now?" Murray Levison asks me. "American flags?"

The King squad, jogging cockily, is on the field. On their helmets: American flag decals. Why? Buzz explains it to me later. "A psychological edge. Hard-hats. Hardnoses. Bring us together." It doesn't register with me. Is there an implication in those American flags that Rye Country Day School is less patriotic than King? Is Rye typical of the effete Eastern liberal establishment while King School of Stamford is closer to the honest, hard-working, middle-class American virtues? I'm not sure. At this point the subtleties of Buzz's psychological assault on Rye evade me. That night David confirms that Rye, too, was bemused by the red-white-and-blue decals on the helmets. "Those guys kept asking, 'Hey, what are the flags for?'" "And what was your response?" I ask. "'Fuck you,' we kept telling them." As good an explanation as any.

King loses the toss. It's Rye's ball on its own thirty after Bobby Fieber's kick. Bobby will not play defense. He will kick and run. He looks big and rugged, with a new 22 on the back of his white jersey. He wears a white horsecollar like David's.

On the first play from scrimmage, Al Hall goes to his strength. Robinson keeps and tries to sweep left end. David, in his stand-up left-end position on the six-man line, fights off a blocker, slams Robinson to earth. It's as clean a tackle as I have seen all year, a professional tackle.

Rye lines up strong to King's right side. Another sweep—the play that netted them 159 yards in the first game. This time Andy Levison moves with the runner, Guarnaccia, and belts him in the midriff. No gain. It's third down and not a yard gained yet. Robinson tries a pass. It's dropped. I see Mike Mori, gutsy, unafraid, chasing the receiver, who is a head and a half taller. Now it's fourth down and not a yard gained against Buzz's "6-2 tackle wide." It's the gapping of the guards that did it, I advise Murray. He looks at me as if I have just offered him advice on a bad stock.

Rye punts. Fieber is back. His first run with the ball. He drops it, recovers. Suddenly we realize why Buzz and David and all the others wanted Bobby to play. He is ripping off huge green chunks of field with twisting, churning runs. The plays are basic—off tackle, inside, starting with blocks by David and Edge, then Fieber is running by himself, a big, strong, determined kid. On the third play from scrimmage, Bobby runs head-on into the Rye captain and lays him out cold. He's through for the game. He'll spend the night in the hospital.

We are screaming like the inmates of Charenton. Murray, Norm Fieber, Rutledge. Even the imperturbable Roy Boe looks aroused. The game is minutes old and Fieber, with assists from Cameron Sillars, has us in their territory. Inspired, Jimmy Wilson fades, throws a pass to Ralph Esposito. Espo makes a leaping catch. It's first down on Rye's thirty-yard line. Now ask us what those American flags are for, you dumb liberals!

Rye starts to stick. Angered by the toughness of the league's weak sister, they hold on at their own twenty-five-yard line. But they are puzzled, frustrated. They take over, and again their running game is a flop. They cannot turn the ends. David is ready for them. So is Edge. The backs run wide, and there are four white jerseys swarming around them.

Across the field, Al Hall is yelling: "What's going on? What's the matter with you guys?" He refuses to accept Buzz's defenses. It's as if a different team—St. Luke's or Cheshire—showed up in King jerseys.

Robinson tries a wobbly pass. Even the rush is better. Mori, looking like the team mascot, intercepts on Rye's forty-one-yard line. Buzz's face is purple with triumph. I wonder: Is he savoring victory too soon? Ah, but he knows something. He knows *we are taking it to them.* He sends in plays, each as bright as a new silver dollar. Fieber twists and squirms nine yards. He breaks three tackles. Sillars slices off tackle for five more. A dump pass, Wilson to Espo, is good for more yardage.

"We are blowing those kids five yards off the ball," Buzz says. "Hall doesn't know what he walked into."

Rye, suffer! Suffer, just for being elitist Rye and all it stands for! I banish from my mind the Jewish names in the Rye line-up, the black scholarship boys. In my dumb euphoria, King has become a force for egalitarianism, the rising of the lower middle class against its WASP masters. (With Vince Lombardi as President?)

The offense, the celebrated "veer," is working as efficiently as a Miami Dolphins play. The running is largely inside; the passes, short. It is ball control at its most beautiful. Buzz calls it "a way of life." *"Our VEER offense is one of patience. It requires testing of the defense to find its weakness. Then we will exploit those weaknesses, which will lead us to VICTORY."* We are watching the words of the master come to life.

On Rye's twenty-yard line and driving, Sillars fumbles after being forced wide. Rye recovers on its own seventeen-yard line. But once more the six-man front frustrates them, all those snooty kids who ran riot over King three weeks ago. Dave wrestles away a blocker and tackles Robinson, who has by no means quit. He wiggles to a first down. The quarter is two thirds over and it is their *first* first down. They try to sweep again. Guarnaccia carries. When the ends are moved out, Mori, ridiculous under a helmet that appears two sizes too big, trips him up. I now understand Buzz's search for "people who like to stick." Mori is one of them.

Another Rye fumble. In their snappy black and gold uniforms, they look worried and hesitant.

It's time to unleash John Daum, the rangy soccer goalie whom Buzz got as a bonus when he persuaded Fieber to play. It's a Stanley special, the flanker pass. Sam Boe moves from his flanking position to behind the center. Wilson takes the snap, fakes, hands off to Boe. Boe fades. The pass blocking is magnificent. Dave, Edge, Andy, and the others form an unbreakable barricade around him. I hear the grunts and gasps of hard contact.

Boe throws downfield, Daum leaps high and catches the ball. It's the first varsity football game he has ever played.

"These kids are great," I say to Norm Fieber and Murray Levison. "They *have* to win this." As I say it, I sense the old pessimistic grayness coming over me. My problem is that I am bereft of belief. Past fifty, one expects less, settles for less.

From the twenty-five-yard line, Fieber runs outside to the Rye eight. The play gathers momentum, comes hurtling toward us on the sidelines with hurricane force. Dave is leading the blocking. His face is rigid with determination. He smashes into a Rye linebacker and sends him galley-west into a knot of spectators.

The quarter ends with King on Rye's five-yard line. There is no question we can win it.

"Your kid makes a difference," I say to Norm Fieber.

"I know."

We stand opposite the line of scrimmage, shrieking for the

touchdown. Sillars goes three yards to the two. We can hear the Rye linebackers exhorting the front to hold. Fieber tries to run outside, but they're ready for him. After all, they are an undefeated team. They have visions of a Fairchester championship. They will not be humiliated by these upstarts. Bobby loses a yard.

Third down. Fieber goes outside again. He seems unstoppable, his powerful legs kicking at tacklers. He needs inches for a first down. Inexplicably, as he is falling forward, he spins, turns, loses a few feet. It's fourth down, still inches for a first down, three yards for a touchdown.

Sillars carries. The Rye line keys on him. No gain.

We blink our eyes, try a few weak smiles, find no words.

"I guess they wanted it more than we did," I say helplessly.

Rye has the ball on the three. Someone fumbles on the ten. King recovers. We can do it now. Buzz calls a play-action pass. Jimmy Wilson fakes nicely, but the rush isn't fooled. He's thrown for a five-yard loss.

Again, I feel shivers of doom in my gut. I have antennae for these awful turns of fate. I am a clairvoyant of disaster. In Europe I often predicted when Marie would lose a purse with our passports and traveler's checks, when our Peugeot would be ransacked, when the landlady would raise the rent.

And it comes. Wilson throws to Boe on the goal line. It is a good pass. The heir to the Nets and the Islanders is there. But Guarnaccia is in front of him. Guarnaccia must be hungrier than Boe. He intercepts and starts down the near sidelines. There is no doubt in my mind. He will go all the way.

Two white jerseys are chasing him. One is Mark Barrett, a new find at defensive back. He is a sophomore, a small, dark boy. Barrett won't quit. He runs parallel to Guarnaccia. One other player is running with him. It's Dave Green.

"Go, 'Mean Joe'!" a cheerleader shrieks.

"Stick him!"

"Catch him!"

Guarnaccia runs on dancing feet. I fear him. Everyone else is out of the play. It's just Guarnaccia, number 11, fast, strong, against Mark Barrett and my son. A ray of hope: Does Guarnaccia suspect that Dave is half-Pomposelli? That the same dark blood runs in his pursuer's veins as in his own?

They will run forever. My heart is a block of ice. My bowels want release. A migraine is coming on. Stanley is racing down the sidelines with them, aggravating his bad knees.

"Get him! Get him!" we scream.

Barrett and Dave converge on Guarnaccia at King's forty-yard line. They time their moves, smash into his legs, knock him out of bounds, roll over him. It is a moment of football perfection—violent, sudden, an explosion of bodies, noise, emotion.

"Way to go, Mark!" I shout. "Good stick, Dave!" I look around for the other fathers. "How about that kid Barrett? And the size of him!"

A teen-age girl smiles at me. "My brother."

I love her. I love Mark. All the Barretts.

Rye tries to penetrate the six-man front with its maddening variations. I see Buzz saluting—the signal for a "storm" stunt. It's David's move. He slants in and levels the runner as soon as he takes the handoff. A four-yard loss. Two more runs are smeared. Rye can't figure out where the defenders will be. I see what Stanley is doing—moving the defensive ends back, forward, shooting linebackers, confusing the blockers.

Rye punts again. Fieber is downed on the five. In desperation a Rye tackler grabs his face mask. Fifteen yards for our side. More short, steady yardage. There's a dump pass to Espo. A long twisting gain by Sillars. A ten-yard run by Fieber. The half is running out and it's still 0-0. A long pass, Wilson to Boe, is incomplete. Jimmy Wilson keeps, runs outside for long yardage, fumbles. Rye gets the ball on our forty as the half ends.

King has made *thirteen* first downs. Rye has made *one*. And the game is scoreless.

"Are they going to do it?" I ask Murray and Norm.

"You bet," says Murray.

"They have to," Norm adds. "They've got those guys demoralized. They're blowing them out of the ball park."

I wonder. The score should be 12-0 King, maybe 18-0. But I fear for our side. In advance, I am contemplating a moral victory.

As the second half opens, Tukes, our only black, gets off a long, twisting runback of the Rye kick-off. It's his best effort of the year. He picks up a short kick, evades tacklers, runs to midfield.

Do we need more blacks? Italians? Poles? I wonder about all the proper WASP names on the roster. Good, willing boys. And only two and a half Italians—Espo, Mori, and Dave.

Ethnic musings are useless. With a suddenness that shocks us, Rye scores. Is it possible King was playing over its head? That the team committed the sin of *hubris* and the gods decided to put it in its place?

Months later, the events still depress me. It is like rereading an old panning review. Fieber goes into one of his mysterious spins and fumbles. Rye gets the ball on King's forty-two-yard line. Eginton gets sucked in (one of the day's rare defensive lapses) and Guarnaccia goes for five. Still no trouble in sight. Guarnaccia goes up the middle for ten. There are other short, inexplicable gains. The defense that worked so beautifully in the first half appears to have forgotten the tricks. Rye is now on King's eighteen-yard line. Dave sticks Guarnaccia on the first play. Then Robinson keeps, evades a tackler, and, as we watch in horror, runs all the way. Boe misses him on the goal line. It's 6-0.

The Rye bench is cheering, leaping, hugging one another. *Villains! Contemptible scoundrels!* Never have I hated a football team so much. *The gall! The arrogance!* They failed to score, got one first down, were made to look like fools for a half. Now, in three minutes, they are ahead.

Robinson tries for the extra points. Dave, whose tackling seems to get better each time I see him, stays with him, belts him to earth. No extra points.

Buzz gathers his team at the sidelines. "Listen to me. We're coming back. We get a TD and the extra point and it's our game. They haven't made a single adjustment. You hear me? Get in there and *stick*."

My long nose is aquiver. We have stopped shouting on the side-lines. The nubile cheerleaders, unbearably pretty, exhort us to urge King on. But the cheers are too long and complicated. Nobody knows them. I slump on the wooden stands and try to hide under my beret. I'm hurting for David, for Buzz, for all these kids trying to bring football back to King School. Why in heaven's name is it so important to me? Why must I bleed when they bleed, suffer when they suffer? And it's no longer just David for whom I weep. It's skinny Sillars with his outraged eyes, lanky Boe, getting racked up, rising to throw again. When Edge gets sucked in or Jimmy Wilson slips, I stumble with him. Andy, Rut, Rag—my heart aches for all of them.

A scream from the Rye side. Something dreadful has happened. A Boe pass has been tipped, intercepted by the ubiquitous Guarnaccia, and he races down to King's twenty-five. It's a forty-yard runback. Eginton stays with him, knocks him out of bounds. I congratulate Margery and Warren Eginton.

We're shouting at King to hold. Twice, they do. But Robinson fakes into the line and runs wide. Sillars stays with him, cuts, falls. Robinson's in for the touchdown. In four minutes of the third quarter, on small lapses, they lead 12-0.

The extra-point try is a replay. Robinson goes wide and into David's 175 pounds. Dave slams the quarterback down.

"You're still in it," Buzz shouts. "Give Fieber downfield blocking and you can beat these guys. They're hurting."

Sotto voce, Buzz mutters to Dave Sample: "Bobby doesn't know where the hell he's going half the time. He didn't even have a chance to learn the plays."

Without downfield blocking, dragging players, Fieber, a bolt of white lightning, carries to Rye's twenty-five. There are short gains. Jimmy Wilson, looking thinner and smaller, is crushed.

Buzz is screaming at the refs for a flag. Piling on. Personal foul. They ignore him. Raging, he throws his clipboard down and breaks it. His papers litter the sidelines. The team manager, Iggy Haims, scampers after plays, defensive alignments.

Fieber fumbles on Rye's twenty-yard line. It is as if the team has a compulsion to lose, is possessed by devils. But the defense will not be moved. Rye's two sudden scoring strikes are all it will allow. I watch David line up in the unfamiliar end-linebacker position Buzz has devised. He follows the flow of the play, wrestles a blocker aside, nails Robinson. There's no more scoring. Twice King moves deep into Rye territory; twice they give up the ball. Raging, Buzz yanks David for two plays after he fails to turn the play in at right angles.

"Big goddamn stud," Buzz shouts at my son's agonized face. "Big hero trying to crash. You were a mile out of position, and he went for ten yards."

David takes it and swallows. I see his tortured face under the helmet. He knows they are losing. Are there tears welling in his eyes? How can I help him? What can I say?

"You want to play, get back in there," Buzz says. "You don't want to play, go to the locker room. Suck up your guts and play football." David runs back in. For two plays, Fieber, the treasure of the offense, was at defensive end. He had not the faintest idea what to do. David tells me he prayed that no play would come his way.

The game grinds to its conclusion. Moral victories are the worst kind. Rye tries to drive again, but its passing game is inept. Mori and Barrett are knocking down passes. Dave, Andy, and Edge lead the pass rush.

It ends in a mishmash of colors, sounds, images. There are grunts and screams, curses, the pounding of cleats on the soft turf. Bobby Fieber, writhing, churning, goes for eight yards. Daum catches a pass. Fieber spins out of bounds. It's too late. The clock is moving, and I am glad. How long can this miserable band of fathers endure the infliction of pain on our sons?

At the final whistle, Fieber is still spinning and twisting. It's no use. We made twenty-one first downs. They made six. And what has it gotten us?

I am enraged at Rye for tossing their helmets into the air, for shouting their triumph. *Some triumph!* They were never in the game except for two freakish sequences. They were humiliated, blown out, dominated, obliterated, creamed, buried. And yet they won. And they have the nerve to act as if it were a great victory.

The white jerseys, dirt-smeared, sweat-soaked, cross the field to offer reluctant handshakes to Rye. David will play no more against Robinson and Guarnaccia, have no more chances to stick them.

Buzz is talking to the Rye coach. "Good game, Al."

"Your guys were great, Buzz. Where'd you get that number 22? He's the best runner we've seen all year."

"He's good."

They part. Buzz turns to his assistants. "I coached Al Hall right out of his shoes. He never knew what hit him." There's a catch in his voice.

Dave Sample shakes his head. "Fumbles. Penalties. Choke-time. We get inside the twenty and something happens."

"It won't next week."

Murray, Norm, Jack Rutledge, Warren Eginton, and I try to comfort our sons. A great game. Beat the hell out of them. They took us 42-0 last time. We damned near won this time. They'll respect us. There's always next week. Kill Hamden Hall.

David turns his back on me. I can't help him. I can't make blocks and tackles for him.

Buzz Stanley puts his arm around David's shoulders. "Good game, Mean Joe. It could have gone our way."

I feel he's telling him that to make up for the bad game David had against Deaf. But David doesn't seem to hear. His eyes are misty and I cannot bear to look at him. Dimly, I see him in a droopy pair of yellow bathing trunks, age one and a half, climbing into a backyard pool in Westbury. Brown, undersized, thin, pot-bellied, furious at being shoved aside by his older brother and sister.

"Does it hurt, Murray?" I ask Levison. "Do you feel as bad as I do?"

"Every bit as bad, Jerry. I need a few fast Scotches to make it go away. Those poor kids. Andy is crushed."

Me, I don't even have the consolation of a drink or two. Migraine keeps me from alcohol. Like Harry Hope, I've discovered there's no life in the booze.

At night, shaved, lotioned, full of aches and honor, Dave is off to the postgame bash at Rutledge's. I stop him at the door and mumble some words of good cheer. "Okay, okay, I know all that," he snaps. "Will you cut it out?"

I've located something in Walt Whitman that I hope will raise his spirits. "A great poet, Dave," I say, as he stands impatiently at the garage door. "Listen to this."

And I read:

> I play not marches for accepted victors only.
> I play marches for conquer'd and slain persons.
> Have you heard that it was good to gain the day?
> I also say it is good to fall, battles are lost in the
> Same spirit in which they are won.
> Vivas to those who have failed.

He shakes his head in disbelief. "Boy, what an attitude. If I showed that to Buzz he'd kick my butt."

"You played well. You have nothing to be ashamed of in losing."

But he's gone. It's his life, and maybe I'm wrong to try to console him. Besides, what did Walt Whitman know about the 6-2 tackle wide?

7

"Mr. Stanley made me a nose guard."

"Oh? Plastic?"

We're at the dinner table. A cold October evening. David averts his head—disgust at my ignorance. Or does he think I'm joking? I'm not. I assume you *wear* a nose guard. His room is a bat's nest of armor—varieties of jocks, guards, protectors. Before hockey games he spends an hour girding himself, like a medieval knight prepping for a tournament. I have the feeling he has to be lifted by a gantry into his goalie pads.

"You don't wear it, Dad. It's a position."

"No more linebacker? Or that crazy six-man front with you and Edge on the ends?"

Marie pays no attention. Normally she spends dinnertime trying to draw him out. Both our sons value silence. But if the talk is of football—or hockey, or tennis, or skiing—she opts out. Is she bothered on these evenings by the same autumnal musings that render me somber and meditative: the stabbing thought that in a year David will be gone, along with the other children, and we will be alone, staring at each other over the minestrone, searching for words after the last stuffed calamar' has been eaten?

"Mr. Stanley says we were scouted. Besides, the five-man front should stop Hamden Hall. Mr. Kelly scouted *them*. They run from a wishbone with the second man through. And they have one good pass play. He figures I can clog the center up."

"I see. Nose guard: I like the sound. You prefer it to line-backer?"

"Yeah. I'm right in the middle of everything. Head to head with their center. I can stick his ass every time."

"David!" Marie cries.

But I am convulsed with laughter. It isn't much of a line—the literary level of sports jargon isn't very high—but I love it. Never have I had the opportunity to stick an opposing center's ass.

At night I descend to the basement to see how the Bitonto Cathedral is coming along. According to my sources, the original took twenty-five years to build. A gem of Norman Romanesque in southern Italy. We'll knock it off in a few weeks. Dave is still sawing sections out of the plywood. Marie and I will help him design the cutouts he'll glue on. One problem: there's no drawing of the apse. I'll have to look through other reference books in my collection, but none of them is very helpful on southern cathedrals. (Because, Marie says, they are all written by nothern Italians, who regard the south as a land of Arabs and Greeks and Africans. She has taken on many an uppity Milanese in her day. In a sense, she is a kind of nose guard herself, in behalf of southern Italians.)

In between discussions of the clerestory and the west porch, David tells me about the upcoming game with Hamden Hall. Originally, this Saturday was supposed to be an off date for the team. The regular Hamden Hall game is to be at King a week from Saturday. But Buzz could not bear the idea of an open date. Moreover the team had almost beaten Rye. It was *developing*. It would surprise the league. So an extra match was scheduled.

"What kind of team is Hamden Hall?"

Dave measures the drawing in the book so he can duplicate the pilasters on the façade. He bends to his work. "We heard they were almost as bad as us, that they might not even have a team. But they lost to Rye by one touchdown, and then almost beat them."

"You almost beat Rye."

"Mr. Stanley says they're big and tough. Their line outweighs ours and they have a good quarterback. Joe Fasano."

Fasano. Is he from Bitonto? Do his antecedents come from a hill town in the Lucania, like Marie's? I leave David to his sawing and measuring and, with a middle-aged man's plodding step, go upstairs. The wind is rising, Bitonto Cathedral is being built, and I fear Joe Fasano. Why does Buzz Stanley have to schedule extra games? I want the season to end. I wonder if I might have been better off languishing in the Philippines, missing all these painful Saturdays. Years ago Lou Little's wife wrote a book about the torments of being a coach's wife. It was called *I Die Each Saturday*. Mrs. Little, meet Gerald Green.

Before retiring, David checks out our medicine cabinet (cabinet? *warehouse* is more apposite) for an Ace Bandage. He has a charley horse. He notices a bottle of Darvon. "Mr. Stanley goes through a bottle of those in three days," he says.

"Nerves?"

"Pain. His knees kill him. Ever since he hurt them in college. The pain doesn't stop."

In my tremulous brain, I see David on all fours in the dirt and muck, a nose guard now, head to head with the Hamden Hall center, new at his position, aggravating the Osgood-Schlatter's disease that lumped his own knees in eighth grade. But I say nothing. Marie has entered the bedroom. It is just as well that Buzz Stanley's ruined knees be kept from her. She will have one more reason for detesting football.

Alone, I drive to New Haven on Saturday. I've played sloppy tennis in the morning. My game will never get any better. Worse —I seem to be dropping in class, moving into a circle of *schleppers* and pushers. The hard hitters gave up on me long ago, and even my peer group, the steady "B" players, look away when I show up in my droopy shorts. I try not to let it bother me. After all, it's the exercise that counts.

It's a rainy day. I stop at a roadside restaurant outside of New

Haven for a meatball hero and coffee. I'm the only customer. The waitress is in her middle fifties, gray-haired and stunning. Where do all these good-looking women come from? She wears her hair piled high, full of lush loops and waves. Gold earrings, artful make-up, lovely bearing, a handsome bosom and a proud behind. All in a starched white pants suit. She is far more exotic than the insipid red sauce on my meatball hero, and she has an engaging way of dropping her final *g*'s as she commiserates with me on my son's football season.

"Where they playin' the game?" she asks.

"In the park. Place called Rice Field."

"Well, good luck. I hope your son finely wins one."

"I hope so too. The meatballs were delicious." They weren't, of course. In no class with Marie's or my mother-in-law's, but I'm perpetually grateful for politeness. Is it because of the impending violence that I must witness? The crack of bodies, the pain, injuries, humiliation?

The King team, in sparkling white jerseys, looks good as it works out. Buzz has some new plays built around Fieber. He has devised a slot formation and a quarterback-in-motion series, all aimed at taking advantage of Fieber's running. John Daum is again playing as a wide receiver. So the offense should be moving. And a face from the past has shown up: a powerful, fair-haired boy named Jeff Gross, whom I remember from David's sixth- and seventh-grade teams. Gross was fast and strong. But his knees have been repeatedly injured. This year it was assumed he could not play again. Now he has pleaded with his parents, with Buzz, to be allowed to suit up. It's questionable whether he'll get in. His presence may have an inspirational effect on the squad. Buzz is a believer in a show of strength. ("Eight or nine of those kids can't be allowed on the field, but it's good to have them in uniform anyway.")

I look for number 51: *the nose guard.* David looks tense, shrunken. (He keeps losing weight throughout the season, although Buzz still insists he weighs 191.) Hamden Hall wears bright green and yellow uniforms. The colors seem to have been borrowed from the Oakland Athletics. They look huge. All of King's opponents look huge. A result, I suppose, of my habit of staring too long at little people like Mori and Barrett.

By now I am identifying with all of the embattled King boys. I can tell Andy Levison's broad back, Eginton's square determined face, Rutledge's looming bulk, Boe's angular form, and, of course, Sillars with his storklike gait. They're my boys. I bleed not only for David Nicholas Green but for all of these diehards with their 0-4 record. *The boy who won't be beaten can't be beaten,* Buzz says. Yes, yes. But a break now and then?

The sun is strong. The field is damp. It's a beautiful park—rocks, old trees, lush turf. The cheerleaders are there again, teasing me with their nude knees, a flash of panties.

Hamden Hall gets off a short kick. Eginton downs the ball on the forty-yard line. Then I notice something strange. Fieber is not in the starting backfield. He's on the sidelines—big number 22, swinging his mighty arms, talking to Buzz. Chris Sweet is deep with Sillars. It's explained to me later: Buzz wants to confuse them. They hadn't scouted the second Rye game and perhaps had not heard about the new star.

But even without Fieber, King is running its lovely "veer" offense. A Wilson pitch to Sillars is good for nine. Wilson keeps for six. Sillars for nine. They are blasting the green-and-yellow opponents yards away from the line of scrimmage. There is an electric shock as Dave, Edge, Andy, Rut, and LeBlanc crash into the defenders. It's pure *veer,* exploiting weaknesses, moving away from strength.

Enter Fieber. Hamden Hall is unprepared for the cyclone. Optimism bubbles in us as Fieber rips off tackle for seven yards. Sillars gains six. Fieber eleven more. In desperation Hamden Hall goes offside. It's first and ten on Hamden Hall's eighteen-yard line.

A beefy man with black, brush-cut hair is seated next to me. He is heavy-jowled, blue-eyed, wears a black-checked apple-green lumberjacket with an American flag perched in a button-hole. "Those kids can *hit*," he says. "They run up the middle like a pro team."

I'm too excited to do more than nod in agreement. It is amazing. Not a single sweep, no end run, not a pass. It's all punishing, straightaway football, hard blocks tearing holes in the line. Buzz is a prophet: *Veer* will succeed.

"Go, Bobby, go!" I shriek.

Norm and Sylvia Fieber are on the sidelines, shouting at their son. He's squirmed to the nine-yard line, carrying four green-and-yellow players on his back.

Hooray for Fieber! Hooray for Sylvia and Norm! I'm grateful to them for having a son like Bob. But why is the referee marching backward? Fifteen yards against King for holding. My heart begins to rise into my esophagus. *Please, God, not David.* Not again. It's a coward's admission, but I'm glad it's Andy Levison who held Hamden Hall's linebacker.

"Too bad," my brush-cut friend says. "Those kids were socking it to them. I like a team likes to hit. Go up the middle. Plain football. Knock 'em down. Blow 'em out."

On the sidelines, Buzz is doing *entrechâts*. Do his knees hurt? Iggy Haims stands by, ready for the clipboard to go again. No. Too early. We're barely into the first quarter.

It's second down and twenty-five on Hamden Hall's thirty-three-yard line. A Wilson pass is short. Sometimes I wish Jimmy didn't throw those flat-handed passes. Fieber grinds for six yards behind David. Hamden Hall has been toughened by the penalty. They know it was a break. They were being devoured, crushed. Another pass is incomplete. The drive ends with the ball on Hamden Hall's twenty-seven-yard line as Fieber is stopped again.

"The guys in white'll kill 'em," my brush-cut American says. "I'm out here every Sat'day. Know all the coaches." He looks Irish or Scotch-Irish—pink skin, black hair, sharp blue eyes. His chest is enormous. I'm sure he bowls. An old local football hero?

Hamden Hall takes over. I'll get to see the nose guard in action for the first time. The first play goes so fast I can barely follow it. Fasano hands off. In a fraction of a second I see Dave's white helmet and the writhing red 51 dart past the center and the defensive tackle, embrace the runner, smash him to earth.

"Look at that 51," my friend says. "Some tackle."

"My son. First time he's played nose guard."

"He's got the moves."

Once again Hamden Hall tries to run at the center of the line. My new friend and I see David hurl himself between blockers, stitch the ballcarrier to the ground. A third run at the line: Fasano keeps, is hugged by five white jerseys. They have moved not an inch in three tries at the King line. Hamden Hall punts. Boe is tackled on his forty-three-yard line. Back to work. We can run against these people. They cannot run against us.

"Your son, huh?"

"He's captain."

Wilson is intercepted. Fasano is a good quarterback. He knows he will have trouble with the middle of the King line. Why not try the ends? A few passes? He starts nibbling at yardage. A run around left end, two more off tackle, a short pass. King is charging, hitting hard. Then Sillars fails to cover a flat pass. Hamden Hall is down to the King twenty-one. Another pass. A lateral. They're on the eight. I'm convinced now they're a better team. The scouting reports were inaccurate.

Fasano fakes, keeps, turns an end. It's 6-0. Seconds later he repeats. Now it's 8-0. Another dose of wormwood and gall.

"How did that happen?" I ask the world. "How did they score so fast?" My mind rejects defeat, the impertinence of Hamden Hall. We are in for another unreal afternoon, a game of nightmares, things that never happened, surrealist nonevents.

"Ran the ends," my friend says. He extends a huge corded hand. His name is O'Dowd, a local citizen. Never misses a game. His favorite high school team is playing away today, so he is at Rice Field. "Played a lot of football myself. U of B."

"Boston?"

"Bridgeport."

I study his lumberjacket, his American flag, his white socks, his polished black shoes. He is perfect in a way I will never be. Mr. O'Dowd of New Haven. What does he do? How does he vote? How does he feel about long-haired students at Yale? Kingman Brewster? Robert Brustein?

We're chopping out chunks of yardage again, the veer shoving Hamden Hall into its cleats. The King offense is like a powerful, flawed engine, starting, jerking, grunting, falling short of top performance. A gear breaks, a gasket blows. The gains are small, exhausting. Sillars for five. Fieber for six. Fieber for five.

David leads the blocking. I see his maroon 51 cut down a linebacker. Fieber is loose. Open field ahead.

Norm and Sylvia are shouting. The cheerleaders are bobbing like marionettes. Buzz is running with Bobby. The fullback is racing in the open with great strides. Tacklers bounce from his legs. On the Hamden Hall twenty-one-yard line the safety man makes a saving tackle.

"Go get 'em, King!" I shout.

"Ram it down their throats!" Mr. O'Dowd says.

I don't know why he's rooting for King over a local school. Maybe to cheer me up. I've told him about the 0-4 record. He knows my son is the team captain. But does he know I voted for McGovern?

Now I fear that Buzz is going to the well too often. They keep giving the ball to Fieber. Hamden Hall is keying on him. He chews his way forward through a mass of flailing, grabbing bodies—three yards, two yards, two yards. Daum is offside. We're back on the nineteen-yard line. Wilson drops back to pass. Fieber catches it. But it's good for only a yard. I learn later that he ran the wrong pattern. Who can blame him? Only two weeks with the squad, carrying the offense single-handed.

Hamden Hall takes over. They can't gain an inch. Enraged, the King front charges furiously. Andy Levison piles up Fasano. David, nose to nose with their center, blasts the second back through. At the half they're deep in their own territory, looking helpless but leading 8-o.

"The way you guys are killing them you should be up 60-o!" Buzz says, as the team heads for a shady knoll at halftime. There is no locker room. "You men have no character. You men are losers. If you guys don't start playing football I'll give you practice after the game."

David looks at me helplessly as he walks by. His brown head rises out of the white shirt, horsecollar, shoulder pads. His eyes plead with me. *Daddy, do something.* He could be five, begging me to catch him a fish at Fire Island. "We're blowing them out."

("I know, son, I know," I want to say. "Keep blowing them out. Something your father could never do.")

Someone tells me that David had seven unassisted tackles in the first half. Iggy Haims, spying on the Hamden Hall bench, reveals that their coach is going to put two men on David in the second half. "Who the hell is that 51?" Coach Jim Bean keeps shouting. "Keep him out of the backfield! Can't you people stop a man from getting through?"

"Dave's up for this one, Mr. Green," Iggy tells me, hurrying to the meeting on the knoll.

"We'll get 'em in the second half."

They call him Iggy after Ignatz Mouse. Mr. Draper, a King teacher, decides that Danny Haims looks like Ignatz. He doesn't really, he's a good-looking boy, funny, busy, resourceful. He mixes a hearty Gatorade and is an accomplished taper.

I wander around, assure the Fiebers that we're going to win it, and return to my seat next to Mr. O'Dowd.

"That kid of yours," he says. "I love a kid who hits. He puts on ten or fifteen pounds I can help him at U of B. I do a lot of recruiting there."

Flattered, I thank him. A satisfying glow warms my chest. Mr. O'Dowd is accepting me into a superior America to which I've never belonged. Why not Bridgeport? Years ago a Stamford school official established a criterion for a new superintendent of schools that he *not be associated in any way with Harvard or Columbia.* It made a headline in the *Advocate,* and I brooded for days. Apparently no one objected. I wanted to call up Jack Arbolino at the College Boards and ask him to apply for the job so I could say to the man, "Here, you idiot, here, you prejudiced dolt, is a Columbia graduate, with two degrees, a Phi Beta Kappa key, a former associate dean at Columbia, who was a Marine hero with more medals than you can imagine, played football for Lou Little, was raised in the streets of the Bronx, and is twice the man that you are. Now, I dare you to challenge his patriotism!"

Oh, dear God, how we are ruled by stereotype! I want so badly to be accepted by Mr. O'Dowd (who occasionally gives me a sidelong glance as if puzzled that someone like me could produce a nose guard). As the teams return for the second half, he's into a long story that I can't quite follow. It's about Earl Warren. Not a dirty story, an angry story. Something about Earl Warren coming to an affair in Bridgeport, and how he, O'Dowd, was chosen to drive the Chief Justice's car, and how he hated every minute of it. "Had to smile at the bastard," Mr. O'Dowd whispers, "and he was the one responsible for everything wrong with this country." I mumble something noncommittal. (Marie would have taken him on, three out of five falls to the mat. But then, she has credentials —the policeman father, the patriotic Pomposellis.)

LeBlanc kicks off. Hamden Hall gets the ball on its own twenty-three. David's white helmet gleams in the middle of the line. My head is fuzzed—my Bridgeport friend's admiration of my son, his hatred of Earl Warren. Where does it leave me? I excuse myself, wander around the field, watch Fasano try the center of the King line again. It's useless. Dave, Andy, and Rut pile them up.

I'm in back of the Hamden Hall bench. Their coach is concerned. They lead, but they have been shoved all over the field. "Where did Stanley get that 51?" he shouts. "Can't anyone lay a hand on that guy?"

He asks an assistant how come the scouting reports didn't tell them about 51. I look at the field again. Another unassisted tackle.

David is playing nose guard the way Rostropovich handles a cello. He gets down low. He's nose to nose with the center. At the snap, he glides or slithers around the center, bypasses the tackles. It's as sweet as a service ace.

The crunch and pop of armored bodies intoxicate me. The runner gets a bare yard beyond the line of scrimmage. Dave has him in a warm hug. They tumble together. Fourth down and seven yards to go. King is holding.

I walk back to our side of the field and Mr. O'Dowd in time to see Jimmy Wilson fumble the punt on his twelve-yard line. By now I am resigned to defeat. What can Buzz be thinking? How can he accept these interminable errors?

"Your boy was in on three tackles in a row," O'Dowd says. "That's some number 51."

"I think he likes the position."

But to what avail? Hamden Hall tries to run and again David leads the charge against the center of the line. On third down Fasano throws a pass to a big end. They're on the King thirteen, fourth down and a yard to go. Once more Fasano fades, throws. Jimmy Wilson plays it cool, cuts in front of the receiver, intercepts on the three. Shouldn't he have batted it down and taken the ball at the thirteen?

It's King's ball on its own three-yard line. It could be worse. There's always Fieber to run them out of danger. Boe carries for no gain. Time-out to regroup.

What follows is one of those mind-numbing irrational tricks of fate or erratic judgment or bad luck that dog the team all year. I sense disaster in my fevered bones when I see what is going on.

Buzz is sending in Jeff Gross. For several weeks Gross has suited up, worked out with the team, but has had no contact. Now he goes in to the backfield alongside Fieber. What is Stanley up to?

LeBlanc snaps. The play is a simple 28 power off tackle with Gross carrying behind Esposito and Levison. It happens so fast I barely can make sense out of it. The next thing I see is a horde of green-and-yellow jerseys (how I hate them!) dancing joyfully. The official is holding pointed hands over his head.

"Safety," O'Dowd says. "They tackled the kid in the end zone."

It's 10-0. How? Why? Poor Gross! His one appearance of the year!

The King team looks stunned. They mill around. Dave and Le-Blanc are shouting at them to get it together. I feel leakage in my coronary arteries. I'm slowly dying. Air! *Air!* I want to go out on the field and destroy someone.

Later it's explained to me. A perfect play. Hamden Hall would expect Fieber to carry the other way. But the blocking fell apart. Crocker, Hamden Hall's all-league tackle, got through and followed. Gross, unable to penetrate, ran wide. Before he could get out of the end zone, Crocker tackled him.

It's the last game I'll attend. I can't digest any more of this. Not at my age, overweight and prone to migraine. There are other things to do on Saturday afternoons in October and November.

We're in the fourth quarter and we're down 10-0.

After King's free kick, Hamden Hall tries to run again. Will they ever learn? David makes two more unassisted tackles. They don't understand the power of a nose guard.

"I got a boy of my own," O'Dowd says to me. "Bigger than you."

"Oh?"

"Seventeen. Six-four, two hundred and thirty pounds. Made him go out for football but he quit. He doesn't like the contact."

"Football isn't for everyone," I say smugly.

Mr. O'Dowd's blue eyes are hurt. His jaw, wider than the brush-out top of his skull, moves laterally. "Don't know what's wrong with him. Quit the team both years. What natural talent. Powerful kid. Fast. But hates contact. His goddamn hair is down to here." He indicates a point three inches below his pink ears. "All the kid cares about is cars and that lousy music they play."

"Well . . ."

"*Your* kid, now. Look at him stick that guy. Came right through the hole. What's he weigh?"

Pride chokes me. I can't take advantage of the man. But I am forced to parade my Americanism. "The program says one-ninety-one, but he's closer to one-seventy-five."

"He does it on guts. I love a kid who can stick."

Levison and Edge pile into the runner. Hamden Hall fumbles. Someone recovers on the King forty-two. There's time left for a miracle. It comes from Sam Boe. Coach Stanley's weird "quarterback in motion" series confuses Hamden Hall. Wilson shifts. Boe moves over from his flanking position, takes a direct snap. He completes a pass to Daum, another to Wilson. Then a flare pass to Fieber and a first down. It's not too late. It never is. When the team was down 42-0 against Rye, Buzz was calling time with a minute left, determined to score. Now he wants to win. I believe in him. It can be done. Boe shifts, takes the snap. The blockers form a wedge around him. I see Dave, Andy, Edge, and LeBlanc fighting off the rush. They look weary. The pass is a jewel—high, spiraling, rich brown against the blue October sky. Daum leaps and catches it on the seventeen-yard line.

There's a minute and twenty-six seconds left. Where did the time go? Next play: Fieber off tackle.

"Go, Bobby, go!" Norm Fieber is yelling.

Bobby goes. He's dancing a solo, a wild ballet. He rips off nine yards. Players slide from his legs. He flattens a linebacker.

Quarterback in motion. Boe moves over. The defense shifts, expecting the pass again. But it's a simple 29 pitch. As Wilson moves left, Boe pitches to Fieber, who goes the other way. Sillars and David lead the blocking. Huge Crocker stands in their way. Dave, outweighed by twenty pounds, levels him. Fieber dances into the end zone. It's 10-6 with less than a minute to go.

The extra-point play is more pure "veer." Wilson fakes, moves right, goes in standing up. We trail 10-8.

There are fifty-eight seconds left. LeBlanc's onside kick almost works, but it squirts away, and the opponents have it on their own forty-three. King holds them again, gets the ball back. With thirty

seconds left, a desperate pass by Espo on the end-around is intercepted. It's over.

"You have nothing to be ashamed of," Mr. O'Dowd says. "Nice
meeting you, Mr. Green." He crushes my wet hand. Does he comprehend the sorrow filling my heart? Maybe, maybe not. He has a
230-pound son who won't play football.

I can't get myself to go down to the field. What can I say to the
team? Fumbles. The safety. Poor Jeff Gross in for one play—and
disaster. The boys are dragging themselves across the field to the
yellow bus. Halfhearted handshakes with the Hamden Hall players, who seem almost ashamed to have won. They know they have
been drubbed. Later I hear the statistics: Hamden Hall four first
downs, King *nineteen*. Yards rushing: Hamden Hall 78, King 253.
All afternoon I have watched Bobby Fieber running through
green-and-yellow jerseys. David slamming down green-and-yellow
jerseys. And still they have lost.

Nearing the bus, I try to say something to a furious David, a
solemn Edge, a stunned Sillars. Silence. I can't find the words.
Finally I choke out something inept. "Tough game. You'll get
them next week. They don't belong on the same field with you."

On the last sequence of plays, I overhear someone say, Sillars
stuck Fasano so hard he broke his own face mask. Small consolation.

"We beat the piss out of them," David mutters. There is a crack
in his voice. Sixteen unassisted tackles. He will be named athlete
of the week by the coaches. Jim Bean will spend the next six days
devising defensive strategies to keep him out of the Hamden Hall
backfield.

The yellow bus chugs away into the tree-lined road that winds
through the park. I look around for someone to share my misery.
The Fiebers have gone. My friend O'Dowd has vanished. Back to
Bridgeport and his bowling club.

It's wrong for me to be exhilarated, but as I walk to my car, listening to the happy shouting of the Hamden Hall team, it dawns

on me that something strange and mysterious has happened to me that October afternoon. *I have become an American, at age fifty-one. My son has made me an American.*

The Bridgeport exits on the turnpike, the grimy smokestacks and hideous red brick buildings (blacking factories? sweat shops?) remind me of my friend Mr. O'Dowd and his admiration for David's performance. Fair enough. But what about me? What does it do for me?

Without David, what would I be to O'Dowd *if he really knew?* Give him a blank sheet, let him fill in the details. Here I am, O'Dowd, the enemy of the people. Liberal. Writer. Media man. McGovern-backer. I am in favor of legal abortion and of gun-control laws. I believe in the Miranda decision. As a matter of fact, I admire the late Chief Justice Warren.

And you, sir, with your shaved head and flag and guns and bowling league and Bridgeport. You can beat me every way I turn. You can win elections forever. You count more than I do. Your vote is more precious than mine, because there are so many of you.

But who shook *my* hand? Who accepted me because of my son's sixteen unassisted tackles? David will never quite understand. He will never know what status he conferred on me, how he pinned the flag on my lapel, made me acceptable to Middle America, to the American Rifle Association, to all of Bridgeport.

It's as simple as that. O'Dowd's huge son doesn't like to stick or get stuck. But my son enjoys it. Oh, it makes a world of difference. I envision O'Dowd at the next meeting of his bowling team. "I saw this kid play for King, only one-seventy-five but, boy, he can hit. I never saw a guy play nose guard like he does. All over the place. Ten more pounds and I'd get him into U of B. The old man was a pretty nice guy, also."

I'm tempted to start collecting small arms. Shoot deer in the heart. Learn to bowl. Drink rye and ginger ale. But I never will. I'm playing a part. I'm fooling poor O'Dowd, but I love every minute of it. No apologies to anyone any more. Sir, I am an American. Don't question my patriotism. Don't call me an effete Eastern liberal or a Nixon-hater. Find me a right-winger with a son who plays nose guard the way mine does, then I'll talk to you.

Approaching Stamford I am reminded of a middle-aged fellow I used to meet on the train some twelve years ago when I was commuting to New York daily. Boyle? Doyle? Tall, gray, with outraged eyes and a loud voice. He read *National Review*. We had mutual friends. He was not quite a John Bircher, but close enough for discomfort. He wondered who had taken *In God We Trust* off the dollar bill. Digging me slyly in the ribs (he was strong, too) he would say, "We know, hey, Green? *We* know who did it." He referred to FDR as the Mad Monarch of Hyde Park and to Mrs. Roosevelt as Big Mouth.

I hated and feared him. Because I barely knew him, I did not argue with him, nor did I encourage his friendship. Usually our mutual friend, noting my embarrassment, would take up the debate in behalf of embattled liberal causes.

Now I have a wild impulse to look up Coyle or Foyle or whatever his name was. Ring his doorbell. Confront his angry face and say: "Boyle? Green here. Remember all that crap you gave me on the New Haven about how Roosevelt was a Commie and Eleanor slept around?"

No response. He moves away. He hides the copy of *American Opinion* he has been reading.

"I've come to tell you my son plays nose guard. He made sixteen unassisted tackles and is tougher than you. Say one word about my patriotism *now* and I'll ram that scandal sheet you're reading down your craw."

I'll never do it, of course. But it's a good feeling. If only Dave and his team could feel so good after a game. Just once, dear Lord.

8

Under the sepulchral basement lights, the Cathedral of Bitonto is beginning to rise on our sagging Ping-Pong table.

The façade is splendid. So are the side walls. But there's no apse.

"No apse?" I ask David.

"I can't find a picture of it."

"We'll fake something. Apses are round."

"How do I cut something round out of plywood?"

"We'll use cardboard." I help him make tracings on the white cardboard we'll paste over the plywood. I wish the book had a better drawing of Bitonto Cathedral. He chose it because the lines looked simple. Also because it seemed obscure. He figured that Notre Dame or Bruges or Orvieto would be open to challenge. Mrs. Eastman, the art history teacher, is less likely to be an authority on Norman Romanesque.

Marie joins us, offers some criticism of the transept. Why are we so involved with Bitonto Cathedral? We know. David is the last of the children; he'll leave soon. Who will mow our lawn? Watch the Knicks with me? We grasp at the plywood church because it reminds us of Italy, where we spent two shimmeringly wonderful years. Nancy was seven, Ted five, David three. I give David the cutout for one side of the church. He matches it against plywood, trims it. It's three days after the Hamden Hall game. Buzz has gone easy on practice. He's confident of victory this Saturday.

"They're hurting so bad they don't want to play us again," David says. "We creamed them."

Again, I'm ashamed of my compulsion to encourage this game of violence. But I can't help it. Is it such a jump from the wondrous beauty of a twelfth-century cathedral to football? I've read about the Norman knights in southern Italy. Cruelty. Torture. Deception. Physical strength. The stronger swords won it all. Final score, Count Roger: 56, Saracens: 0. Did Roger gap the pikemen and play the crossbowmen deep?

"Didn't I see you smacking one of the linemen on the helmet?" I ask. "Is it legal?"

"You're allowed one hit with your hand on the charge."

"Oh."

"There was this black kid on the line. The first time we lined up he said to me, 'Let's see how tough you are, you MF.' "

"And you . . ."

"I cracked him on the side of the helmet with my hand."

"And then?"

"He called me MF again. Not the initials. Both words. So I hit him again. He wasn't that tough. I dominated him."

"How many times did you hit him?"

"In the first quarter, about twenty. Every time he said it. By the middle of the second quarter he was walking in circles. He couldn't find his way to his own huddle."

"He didn't get mad?"

"Well, he didn't try anything. The main thing was he stopped calling me that."

I leave David studying the ornate doors of the cathedral and trudge upstairs to relate this story to Marie. She is deep into Orton Society publications. She loves her work. Her room is piled high with books, magazines, charts, aids-to-learning. She entered teaching in her forties the way David took to playing nose guard.

"That's a disgusting story," she says. "Why do you keep chuckling? You'll be telling it all over Stamford."

"You should be cheering. Your family are the quintessential blue-collar ethnics who fled the Bronx because of boys who shout MF in the street. Your father favors public execution of rapists. He'd understand David."

"The whole thing is unnecessary, and you're wallowing in all that meanness. I'm sick of your stories about your weak ankles and the games you weren't allowed to play."

"Not to mention the rich girls who spurned me and the headaches I get."

"There you go. Let me read, please."

I won't be deterred. There are subtle nuances in my relationship to David that elude her. "Look, do you know what I would have done if that kid had called me MF? I'd have smiled and in my best liberal manner said to him, 'I know you come from a deprived cultural background and these latent hostilities are perfectly understandable since they reflect your justified anger at the exploiters, and you and your peer group must have a way of acting out your animosities. So you may call me MF all afternoon during this football game, and although I will play hard and fair, I will in no way react to the gratuitous insult. Right on, Brother.' That's how I would have handled it, and I would have hated my gutlessness. David did the right thing."

"I suppose this is the highlight of the season for you?" she asks. She isn't convinced. "Your son beats another boy on the helmet until his head was ringing?"

"The kid asked for it. Black, white, yellow, he deserved the klops." She succeeds in arousing some of my ever present middle-class guilt. No, I tell myself, it isn't *all* my fault. "I accuse you of the murder of Mack Parker," James Baldwin once told a group of white writers. "Not me," Nelson Algren answered, "I was drinking beer on Division Street that night." I can't be as cavalier as that.

Depressed by Marie's inability to share my enthusiasm for our son's display of manliness, I point out to her that David, along with Andy, Bob, and other seniors, spends two afternoons a week off-season tutoring and playing games with black youngsters in a downtown Stamford school. It is, in fact, the school where she teaches the special class. David is a hero to Christopher Suggs, Grover Brown, and James Washington. They listen raptly when he tries to teach them long division or tell them football stories or goes one-on-one with them in the schoolyard. "Where David?" they would ask Marie. "David not comin' today? He really your son, Miz Green?" And one day, Christopher, pathetically: "He live at home with you and his Daddy?" Once David fished a drowning Grover Jones out of a pool, jumping in clothed, bespectacled, wallet in pocket. Grover was ashamed to admit he could not swim. I rattle on like this because, having rejoiced in his forthright response to the lineman's needling, I'm impelled—that old liberal guilt again!—to demonstrate that he gets along with, likes, has no sense of strangeness with, blacks. It's not his fault or mine or Marie's that we've got 350 miserable years of history to contend with.

Hammering from the basement: The master builder is tacking the roof onto his cathedral. I settle into an armchair with Trevelyan's *Garibaldi and the Making of Italy*, but my mind is back in Brooklyn.

Spring day, Brownsville. Sholem Bernstein and I are walking home from Junior High School 210. We're on Prospect Place, two blocks from home. There's a stretch of neat frame houses where black families live. (In those days we called them "colored" or "Negro" or "*schwarzeh*.") Sholem and I are debating whether Glenn Wright or Ossie Slade played more games at shortstop for the Dodgers. Absorbed in our discussion, we pass a group of black children.

Suddenly the black boys have come abreast of us and halt us. Two of them, both smaller than I, one the color of Schrafft's coffee ice cream, one mahogany, grab me. Why not Sholem?

"You the guy called that kid *black?*" the darker boy demands. He points to a four-year-old with wide, fascinated eyes.

"He deh one," the tot says.

"No I'm not. I didn't say a word. I didn't even see him."

Four hands clutch at my lumberjacket. My books fall. Terrified, I look at Sholem, imploring for help. He's neutral. "Tell them," I beg. "I didn't say a word. Why would I call anyone black? I don't even know you fellows."

Bernstein finds his voice. "He didn't say anything. We were talking about baseball."

"He deh one," the infant says. A black finger points at me.

They shake me. I rattle. I don't resist. I don't challenge them to a fight. Who can fight? Besides, these Watusi will eviscerate me and barbecue me. The Washing of the Spears.

"Listen, I have no prejudice. The farthest thing from my mind would be to insult anyone on the basis of his religion or race. I mean it. I didn't say anything to the boy."

The two attackers look at each other with veiled glances. I'm not worth their trouble. Whether it is pure blood sport or the toddler actually thought he heard an insult I never learn. They shove me into Sholem's arms.

"Git the fuck outa here," the beige boy says. "You come hyeah agin, we beat the shit outa you."

For the rest of the school year I find that Park Place is a more interesting street than Prospect Place. Sholem notes my change of route. "You're scared of them," he taunts.

"I admit it. They'd have killed me. A whole gang would have shown up. Would you have fought back?"

"I'd have challenged one to a fair fight."

I doubt it. And I'm silent. I never tell my father. He'd have raged against my cowardice, raised the banner of boxing lessons again. It's a shame he never lived to see David blow men out.

At midweek, King begins to worry. Fieber may not play, may take a trip to look at colleges. Stanley appeals to him: This is the game we will win. Hamden Hall fears him, fears Green, fears all of them.

"As for you, Mean Joe," Buzz tells David. "Bean is sick of you getting into his backfield. He says it's the best he's ever seen any kid play nose guard in this league. So he's putting two men on you, the center and Crocker. On some plays there'll be three men."

"That'll let the rest of our line through."

"They don't worry him. He wants to burn your ass."

"I'm not scared."

Buzz grabs his neck. "They want to show you up. Bean thinks you're one of the two best linemen in the league. Before the season he didn't even know who you were. Oh, they'll be after you, big stud."

I hear the story at dinner the night before the game. As David leaves for some last-minute beer drinking before Buzz's 9:30 telephone bed-check, I become manic. I call my lawyer, my agent, several friends, my brother-in-law. (He played for Boys' High School in Brooklyn in the 'twenties alongside the immortal "Indian" Yablock.)

"The coach of Hamden Hall says Dave is one of the two best linemen in the league," I burble. "How about that?"

Marie takes the phone away. I'm dreaming of headlines.

FOE'S COACH NAMES GREEN
ONE OF TOUGHEST IN LEAGUE

It never occurs to me to ask Buzz who the other lineman is. Fat Charlie Griffiths at 268? Probably. Is it possible Dave can put on another twenty pounds? Thirty?

We're all back to King's field for the second Hamden Hall game. The opponents look cocky, aroused. They seem to be overdoing the pregame drills, as if to give the lie to the rumor that they were reluctant to take on bone-cracking King a second time. (The bone-crackers are now 0-5.) There's a rumor that Coach Bean kept them off contact drills all week.

The corporal's guard of parents is back—Levison, the Fiebers, the Haims, the Egintons, the Rutledges. I'm introduced to a slim, dark man in a white turtleneck. He's John Mori, Mike's father. I tell him how much I admire his son. Mr. Mori is glad to hear it. He's convinced this is the game we'll win.

As usual, we start brilliantly. A textbook offense. Short yardage, cross-blocking. Fieber, Sillars, and Wilson all carry. We're on Hamden Hall's twenty-three. But the veer machine sputters. Twice Fieber is stopped by huge Crocker. There's a busted play, a bad pass. Hamden Hall's ball.

In minutes, Jimmy Wilson intercepts Fasano's pass. We cheer. This will be a different game! King can win the way I win at tennis. (When I do.) Let the other fellows make the errors. Play it straight, close to the vest—and let them throw bad passes.

Dave blocks for Fieber—a long run deep into Hamden Hall territory. The green-and-yellow jerseys litter the field. Wilson is forced outside. He keeps trying to get around his pursuers, but he doesn't have the speed. It's a big loss. On the next play Edge is holding. We're way back on their forty-eight. Fieber gets off a good kick to their sixteen-yard line. No great harm. We've made errors, they've made errors. But there's no doubt which team is tougher.

"Get it back, Andy," Murray shouts to his son.

"Stick 'em, Green," I add.

The nymphet cheerleaders smile at me. Pretty little blossoms! Do they know I am the daddy of fierce 51?

We're still assuring ourselves that this is the big game when Joe Fasano mysteriously runs seventy-eight yards for a touchdown on a roll-out. Poor Ralph Esposito gets sucked in. One defender gone. Cam Sillars, at linebacker, fails to support. He just isn't there. There's nothing but green turf and the end zone. They run over Rutledge for the extra points. We're down 8-0.

"Same old story," Murray says.

"*Our* kids didn't do anything wrong." An evil thought, but which of us has not thought it?

Sillars fumbles on King's twenty-eight. Doom, doom. Each stab of pain in my innards is followed by a bigger one on David's behalf.

Then it dawns on me: *He doesn't want my misery.* He can handle himself. It's I, with my interminable migraines and shortness of breath, who need sustenance. And I get it from him. Watching him stick. Seeing his determination. "A leader," Buzz tells the *Advocate.* "I'm depending on 'Mean Joe' to get things together out there."

He's getting it together now. The nose guard is down on the ground. After Sillars's fumble, Hamden Hall twice tries to hit the center of the line. Off tackle. Second man through. David reads the play, moves to the side, penetrates. A six-yard loss the first time. Four more yards back on the second run. So what if there are two men on him, center and tackle? *Hit center! Strike tackle!* You shall not pass.

"That goddamn 51 again," I imagine Jim Bean shouting.

As the quarter ends, Fasano throws poorly. Wilson intercepts. Something unpleasant is happening on the sidelines. Assistant Coach Kelly has bawled Espo out for failing to box in on Fasano's touchdown run. He's raging at the kid. I never get the story straight. Harsh words are uttered. Tempers rise. Mr. Vance, the headmaster, appears. He's talking to Kelly. Buzz stays away. He's too concerned with his offense. They aren't moving the ball.

King's ball on its own thirty-five. The offense is jerky, erratic. I watch Sillars try the outside. He is fast enough, hard to bring down with his crazy stride, but he won't squeeze the football. It bounces loose. Hamden Hall recovers. I weep for him. Sillars, who calls Dave at midnight to be reassured that it's worthwhile to lose week after week.

Fasano mixes plays. He's small, elusive, handles the ball well. (David tells me he's a good guy, pleasant, not a dirty player, always with a generous word for his opponents after a game.) Taylor, Hamden's running back, makes a few short gains. Before we realize it, they've scored again. Short, modest runs, then one for eleven yards over tackle. It's 14-0 in the first half.

"Should we leave?" I ask Murray, knowing the answer.

"Never. If they can hang in, we can. They're going to win it." Levison, I suppose, is used to looking on the bright side. He deals in stocks and bonds, puts and calls, futures, options. The game to him is like a sales pitch to a customer. He's got to sound optimistic, full of faith, no matter how dreadful the actuality.

David levels Taylor on the goal line with a rattling tackle. There are no extra points. But we're still down 14-0.

Sillars gets off a good runback, skimming the turf to the forty-three.

He and Fieber alternate. Three yards and a cloud of dust. Buzz pulls a fast one. He calls a Boe special. Sam shifts, takes the direct snap, passes sixteen yards to John Daum. It's as pretty as anything the professionals do. At second down on the Hamden Hall thirty-two, Boe throws again. Daum leaps high, grabs the pass, races in the two remaining yards standing up. It's like a Shakespeare sonnet, a Della Robbia plaque, a Palladio arcade. Levison and I hug each other. We're in the game!

Wilson is tackled on the goal line. We lose the extra point. "The option," Norm Fieber says sadly. "He should have pitched out to Bobby." Norm is right. Bob would have made it.

The teams appear to be wary of each other. Hamden Hall remembers the physical drubbing it took last week. King remembers that in spite of the punishment it dished out, it lost. Panic's icy fingers clutch at my heart as I remember one of Buzz's gloomy comments: "We're always a foot away."

The half ends with Sam Boe trying to connect again with high, looping passes. He hits John Daum once for twenty-six yards, but that ends the drive.

On the sidelines, I sneak glances at Roy Boe. What can be going through his mind? Pride and admiration for his son, of course. The kid took a horrifying beating from St. Luke's, but he hangs in. Mr. Boe deals with million-dollar babies like Julius Erving, Denis Potvin. How can he feel about this rinky-dink football team? I'm glad, though, that he's on our side.

Second half: Hamden Hall fails to move, has to kick. The old nose guard is at it again. The center, Yeats notwithstanding, is holding. Apparently no one is calling David MF this time. I squint at the flailing, colliding bodies and do not see his hands cracking against a green-and-yellow helmet. Some sort of racial peace has been achieved; manners prevail.

Fieber's loose. He's running past everyone. Norm and Sylvia, Murray, all of us are screaming. It's a simple 28 power play off tackle. Andy and Espo cross-block, obliterate the line. Sillars is first though. He cuts the linebacker in half. Bobby's legs churn, dig. He may do it all. But the Hamden Hall safety man won't quit. He runs alongside Bob, gets him with a last-second lunge on the twenty-seven.

Twice more Fieber carries the ball for short yardage. Boe throws a short pass to Daum on the five-yard line. They look superb: precision blocking, everyone getting his man. Once more the 28 power slant. Fieber plunges through for the touchdown. It's the kind of sequence they've been capable of all year, had they not fumbled or drawn penalties.

"We'll win this one by twenty points," Norm says. "Those guys will fold."

Dave pulls, erases a linebacker. Wilson tosses to Fieber on the 29 pitch. Bobby steps into the end zone. It's tied at 14-14.

The team from New Haven won't die. Fasano turns end again, races to the King twenty-seven. Soon they're on the fourteen. But the defense turns tougher. Dave penetrates and stops the runner. Another good tackle by Jimmy Wilson, a good stick by LeBlanc. Hamden Hall gives up the ball on King's fourteen as the third quarter ends.

An unfamiliar feeling of optimism pervades me. Norm's right. One quarter left. We're so obviously the better team. One touchdown will do it. Two will be better. Here's the game we deserve, the one we've earned.

We watch, by now convinced that our sons will win. They start a spectacular march from their own fourteen into Hamden Hall territory. The plays are run with snap. Buzz cannot fail. He sends in shrewd, unexpected plays, first with Barrett, then with Boe. The opponents are dazzled.

King is on Hamden Hall's thirty-eight-yard line. Buzz sends in a play he has been saving all season—the *counter bootleg opposite*. The name sends shivers down my spine.

King comes out in a full house backfield. The play is the "full house 19." Jimmy Wilson takes the snap from LeBlanc. He rolls left. The three backs follow him in that direction. Wilson pivots, changes direction, and races toward the tight end's side. He runs without blocking. Dave fights off the linemen. Then he pulls with Wilson and throws a thunderous block against a linebacker who's trying to follow. It's magic. Wilson races nineteen yards, untouched until he gets to the nineteen-yard line.

"A hell of a coach," Norm says.

"Fooled them all the way," Murray says.

But not for long. Wilson rolls again, a variant of the previous play. Crocker breaks through, smashes him, and Jimmy fumbles. Hamden Hall recovers on the nineteen.

We're silent, contemplative. At moments like this I need my daughter Nancy for lessons in transcendental meditation.

Fasano throws a good pass. They're moving to midfield. Will all our calculations go awry? Is Hamden Hall really the better team? Do we delude ourselves through love of our sons?

Maybe not. Wilson, trying to make up for his fumble, sticks Fasano, who drops the ball. We recover.

"Now or never," Norm says.

Murray whispers to me. "I have that feeling, you know? That nothing is ever going to work for these kids. Nothing. It's like the stock market. Nothing we do is right any more. I can't tell my clients that, but I sense it. Just like I keep telling Andy they can win."

"Don't talk about it, Murray. I have the same terrible thoughts, but I never tell Dave. He thought they'd win every game except St. Luke's and Hackley."

"Veer" is working. The old Buzz Stanley punishment. Short yardage, hard blocking, everything contained between the ends. Once more Buzz calls the *fullhouse 19 counter bootleg opposite*.

How do these kids remember all of this? With David smearing the linebacker, Wilson races thirteen yards to the nine-yard line. We'll do it now. We must do it.

Fieber runs wide, gets chased by half the Hamden Hall team, fumbles on the thirteen-yard line. Hamden Hall recovers.

None of us dares to look at Norm or Sylvia. How can we be critical? Bobby's been the bulk of the offense since he came out for the team.

Three minutes left. I find now that I'm praying for a tie. I don't want the win that badly. If I've been guilty of the sin of pride, I'm sorry. Ties are fine. Or at least acceptable.

There's a roughing-the-kicker penalty against us. Hamden Hall gets a chance to move. Mike Mori intercepts a pass over the middle. We're on our own forty-five. Still time. Buzz will pull it out. Long passes by Boe fail to connect. We try the Espo Special—reversing Ralph Esposito, the tight end, and having him throw. No good. Fieber misses a first down by two feet. Hamden Hall takes over. Mercifully, the clock runs out.

A tie. It's like going to the Roxy when you can't get into the Music Hall. Thinking you've hooked a bluefish and coming up with a skate. The boys are miserable. Maybe they're thinking about the missed extra points on the first touchdown. They'd have won it, 16-14.

This time I spare David the clichés. He's cursing under his breath. The Neapolitan blood is boiling. The shadows are dark and menacing on his round face. The eyes are like smoldering coals. Week after week after week—so near, so damnably near.

"I don't believe us," he says after dinner. "I don't believe us. We had nineteen first downs and they had six. We gained 259 yards rushing, they gained 110. And 78 of that 110 was Fasano's run around end. Without that they gained only 32 yards."

"Fumbles?"

"We lost four and Hamden Hall lost two. Our guys choke. That's all there is to it."

"You don't believe that, Dave. You had your bad games."

"*Game.* I stunk against Deaf."

"You'll beat St. Hugh's. You have a chance against Hackley."

"Mr. Stanley says he underestimated St. Hugh's. They're giants. They destroyed St. Paul's. They have a two hundred and forty-pound end."

There's the usual party at Rutledge's that night. To celebrate the tie? When David's gone and I'm alone watching the Knicks, shouting at the TV set as Frazier puts a move on Bing or DeBusschere wrestles his way past Lanier for a rebound, Marie enters.

"Was he all right?" she asks.

"Sure. He's off to the weekly beer bust at Rutledge's. They drown their sorrows in Bud. Did you know that the Rutledges have a black manservant named Ernest? David says he's cool."

"That has nothing to do with what I want to discuss."

"Look at Clyde toss that one in. Off his ear."

"Has it occurred to you that David *hates* football? Hates losing week after week?"

"He loves the contact. He loves to stick. Of course he hates to lose. But the misery doesn't last long. He's young. I lost a lot too, but I got my full growth and earned a living."

"You don't follow me. I think David forces himself to jock around the way he does because of you."

"Great pass, Pearl. Threaded the needle. Sure I have something to do with it."

"You have everything to do with it. He sees you sitting around with your daily migraine, the icebag on your head, popping Cafergot pills, complaining about pinched nerves, muscle aches, stiff joints, canceling tennis games, puffing after you climb our hill, and worst of all, belaboring those old stories about your mother forcing you into Coward shoes, forbidding you to play in the street—"

"I still can't roller skate. I can't ice skate. I'll never learn. It's all passed me by. Nice move, Bradley."

"—and he assumes he's got to prove something."

"In a way you're right. He's sticking for two. He's getting bruised and shook up for both of us. But why fault the kid? He fell into jockery naturally. I didn't force him to play football. Show him a ball and he'll learn to manipulate it. The other day I met Mr. Malloy, his friend Ken's father. We shook hands and Malloy said, 'Say, your boy shoots a great game of pool.'"

"Pool?"

"They've got a pool table. David picked up a cue, and behold—the Hustler. Fast Eddie. Who knows how he learned? It comes naturally to him. Last week after football practice he sneaked out of the house and played two hours of hockey at Crystal Rink. I asked him how he could stand it, and he said it was a light football practice. No contact."

"But does he enjoy all that punishment he takes every week? And losing all the time?"

"Not the losing. But the season's not over. I think if they win one game—just *one*—it'll be a success."

"I hate football. I hate everything about it. And I hate your lunatic cheering. I hate the way you glory in his injuries and the injuries he inflicts on others."

"Let the boy do what pleases him so long as it isn't illegal. Besides he's made me an *American*. It took fifty-one years for me to realize that I am a *bona fide* citizen, a card-carrying, patriotic, United States citizen, who can hold my own with any hard hat, any Bircher, any WASP. Woman, don't you understand that?"

"He'll get injured before the season's over, and it'll be your fault."

"If he didn't get hurt against St. Luke's he'll never get hurt. Two to go, two to win."

I watch Monroe fake, pump, pump again, throw one in from twenty feet. Talk about artistic perfection. Who will watch the Knicks with me a year from now, when David is in college?

9

In my fuzzed mind, awaiting the kick-off for the St. Hugh's game at King School, I find that the past six games (0-5-1) assume literary proportions. They're Norse sagas. Hasidic tales. Legends of the Australian abos. Each game has a distinct quality that suggests a writer or a literary style.

The opener against Rye, so full of confusion, fear, missed assignments, is a Pinter play. There were gaps, silences full of menace. When the linebackers failed to support, you felt it. Terror out of nothingness. Alienation. The inability of men to communicate. The dread inherent in pauses.

St. Luke's was Elizabethan comedy. "La, sir, you make mock of me." The cheerleaders should have been lusty serving wenches, flouncing their skirts at country bumpkins. *A Shoemaker's Holiday; Everyman in His Humor.* How can anyone be serious about a 62-6 loss?

New York School for the Deaf—my son's fall from grace—has to be *Paradise Lost.* Offside on a touchdown, failing to box in, he's Milton's Satan. "Him the Almighty hurled headlong flaming." The heavenly promise of victory, lost forever by dumb football.

The second Rye game? There's tragedy. Here's rue for you. I'm not sure whether it's *Hamlet* or Dostoyevsky. The superhuman effort, the drive to perfection, the mocking of the fates. And then defeat. No, it's Hemingway. It's one of those grand short stories—*The Undefeated,* or *Big Two-Hearted River,* or *The Gambler, the Nun and the Radio.* The kids went down like Hemingway heroes. Battling to the end, almost making it, struggling against the gods, losing, but not dishonored.

The Hamden Hall games are two Sherlock Holmes stories. They are mysterious, unfathomable tales. "I draw your attention, Watson, to the curious incident of the running back in the end zone." Or, "Watson, there's more here than meets the eye. The King School team runs far more plays, gains far more yardage, humiliates its opponents, and in two games can gain only a tie. There appears to be some kind of family curse, some ancient horror at work . . ."

What will St. Hugh's be? Will man, as Faulkner contended, prevail? (Oh, our opponents are men also, but they don't need a victory as badly as we do.) I see St. Hugh's as a terminal struggle of some kind. They're our Everest, our White Whale. This is *Moby Dick.* Buzz Stanley as Ahab. Starbuck, Flask, and Stubb—Green, Fieber, and Levison? St. Hugh's is the great predator of the deep. He will spout black blood for Captain Ahab. We are all aboard a leaky *Pequod,* the frail grandstand.

God has blessed Connecticut today. Clear skies, chilly weather. A civilized place. My eyes are moist. Murray Levison looks at me strangely. "All choked up, Jerry?"

"It's too much. You know that Buzz had those kids working nine hours yesterday to line the field? They painted the end zones. They put in five-yard markers. They painted the goal posts. Buzz says nobody in the world can do up a field the way he can. I want them to win so bad."

"So do I. Andy and Dave left at seven this morning for a two P.M. kick-off. They wanted to psyche themselves up."

I greet Norm and Sylvia, the Haimses, the Rutledges, the Egintons. The diehards. We're still hanging in. A wind is rising, rustling the oaks and maples across the field. The old red and white school buildings have never looked so comforting, so charmingly proportioned.

I interrogate Mr. Vance, the King headmaster, for information on the school. I've no idea how it started, how old it is. He gives me a brochure. Opened in 1876—I like this—"when at the request of several families in Stamford, Mr. Hiram Udall King founded a private school for boys." Now twenty-eight acres and five buildings on the former estate of Richard L. Simon, the publisher. (The boys point out the headmaster's home as the place that once housed Carly Simon; Simon & Schuster means nothing to them.) The school has 316 boys, twenty on full scholarship. The motto: *Veritas et Virtus.* (Yale influence?) There's a rumor that the young Eugene O'Neill was a student at King. Georges Clemenceau taught French at the sister school, Low-Heywood. Lucky Tiger!

In a booklet Mr. Vance gives me is a photograph of the 1876 baseball team. That must be Hiram Udall King himself seated amid these serious boys with the enigmatic legend "Kings 3rds" on their blouses. Mr. King is jug-eared, bespectacled, purse-mouthed. Did they have a winning season? I'm awash with sentiment for these long-departed men of almost a century ago. How innocent the world was! They played their nine innings and were gone.

David and Rag LeBlanc lead the team out. They all look gingery. Roaring, rolling, cracking one another, executing snappy sight-and-sound drills, applauding their own excellence, they seem confident, not at all winless or hapless. St. Hugh's is late. I suspect a trick. They will let King, overpsyched, run itself into a useless frenzy with its workouts.

More bad news. "They're not as punk a team as everyone thinks," Murray Levison says. He tells me about the 240-pound end, a huge linebacker, two good running backs—a black and an Oriental. They demolished St. Paul's of Long Island. They are no longer three-year losers. Buzz, Murray reports, gave the boys the word last night. "You lose this, I'll tear your faces off. This fumbling and choking has got to stop, you understand?"

And it's homecoming day. Buzz has gone all-out: flags, streamers, refreshments. There are tailgate picnics, but I'm too keyed up to accept coffee from Sylvia Fieber. I wander about with Levison, wondering why St. Hugh's is so tardy.

"Maybe they got scared," Murray says. "Buzz looked hard for them. He made them agree to a two-season series. They were only too glad. They don't have a home field, and they knew King didn't have a team last year."

"Where are they?"

"Near Columbia. Maybe some connection with them."

It's a mean thought, but perhaps some of Columbia's hard luck will rub off on this satellite school, if indeed it is one. But they're huge. And they've won already. Where are they? Maybe they'll forfeit. That will surely mean a winless season. I don't kid myself about Hackley. Hackley hasn't won yet, but it plays a fearsome schedule, and it has played close games against powers like St. Luke's, Riverdale, and Cheshire.

"Any new psychological moves from the Buzzer?" I ask Murray.

"The kids have numbers on the *backs* of their helmets. And new American flags."

"Patriotism almost beat Rye the second time. I guess Buzz figures the flag is worth a second try."

Murray chuckles. "Andy says Stanley climbed a tree yesterday. He sent a kid out for flag decals and he came back with the kind you paste inside car windows. Buzz was screaming that they would need transparent helmets to wear them. So he went out and bought the new decals himself."

I wonder about the new jerseys the kids are wearing—white numerals on maroon, a reverse of the standard maroon on white. "Borrowed them from St. Luke's. Dick Whitcomb did Buzz a favor."

David is 50 instead of 51. Andy has a different number. Fieber is still the reliable 22.

"Who got Fat Charlie's?" I ask.

"Rutledge. He was the only one here big enough, and it still floats on him."

Rut looks small in Fat Charlie's tent, number 76. Whitcomb drew the line at letting anyone on King wear Mike Siganos's number 14. Some things are sacred. They'll probably retire Siganos's shirt and put it in a museum at St. Luke's.

"Buzz had other problems yesterday," Murray says. "He and Dave and Andy were marking the field with a special marker the coach rented. It spit up all over Buzz's face. He was raging."

But now Buzz looks cool, firm. His handsome dark head, huge neck, chest, shoulders, arms form a single granite block in a white shirt. No jacket. No sweater. He reminds me of Len Will, the marvelous Columbia fullback of my era, whom I used to see walking in noble silence across the campus, in shirtsleeves on sub-zero February days.

I venture to the sidelines and try to take some photographs of David with LeBlanc and some of the others. "Beat it, Dad, will you?" he growls. "Go away. Just stop taking pictures."

"Why?"

"I'm psyching myself up. I don't want to be distracted."

He's been psyched up since seven that morning. How can they loll around the locker room half the day, waiting, hoping, fearing? Wouldn't it be better to get there just before game time? And where in God's name is St. Hugh's? Have they forgotten? Turned chicken?

Back in the stands, Norm Fieber tells me that Buzz bawled the boys out unmercifully that morning. "These guys are huge. They're mean. They'll kick your ass and blow you out of the ball park. They're up for this. They know we scheduled them because we thought they were losers. That's all changed and you better know it."

There's a vague residue of ill feeling on the squad. The Kelly-Espo-Vance drama of the last game has left lingering rumors of dissension. What really happened? What did Mr. Kelly say to Espo? What did Mr. Vance say to Mr. Kelly? I'm full of sorrow for all of them. For the assistant coach (who could blame him for blowing his stack on Fasano's run?), for Esposito, who's only a tenth-grader and is potentially an all-league end, for Mr. Vance, who has to adjudicate the matter. Some parents heard what was said; noses are out of joint.

I spy a stranger on the sidelines. He's looking for Coach Stanley. Oh, a St. Hugh's person. Eavesdropping, I hear him talking to a controlled but inwardly raging Buzz. "They're on their way," he says. "They should be here in ten minutes or so."

"Why so late?" Stanley asks. "I gave explicit instructions to Coach Valerio."

"Two of the boys were taking their College Boards at Columbia. We had to wait for them."

"Christ, we don't kick off until after three o'clock. An hour late. We'll be playing in darkness in the last quarter."

"I'm sorry, I really am. My boy is on the team and I know they all want very much to play this game."

I case the St. Hugh's parent: bushy mustache, long gray hair, tweedy Irish hat, checkered coat, expensive camera. He has a soft, artistic face. Hardly a man who likes to stick. Hard for me to envision his son sticking. This augurs well. I've learned to fear the spawn of Poles, Italians, and blacks. Dear God, let's have a team of pale scholars, indifferent to the game, weary from the long trip.

Buzz turns to Kelly and Sample. "They're trying to psych us. I had most of the pregame drills on the practice field. Let 'em come as late as they want. We won't leave our game on the field."

As he speaks, a yellow bus arrives in the parking lot. The St. Hugh's team disembarks. I see why Buzz went for the dark red St. Luke's jerseys. St. Hugh's has white shirts. Their helmets are gold and light blue. And they're big.

"Holy God," Murray says. "They're bigger than St. Luke's. Look at that kid."

This must be the giant. He's 6′ 4″. At least 240. A dark, beaked young man. He lumbers across the turf. The helmet looks like a thimble in his hand. He must have destroyed St. Paul's single-handedly.

A nerve-racking delay: St. Hugh's has to practice. They look snappy, professional. At once I begin to worry. Is it possible they'll beat us the way Hamden Hall did? One or two big plays, one good back, while all Buzz's strategy, his multifaceted veer offense, goes for nothing, shattered by fumbles and penalties?

The referee calls the captains for the kick-off. David is a head shorter than the giant. Even LeBlanc, a six-footer, shrinks next to the looming, oversized boy. I know he will be a problem. Is he fast? Does he stick?

The team gathers around Buzz. I hear him say, "The white jerseys make them look bigger. Stick it to them from the start. They'll fold."

As the King team runs out to receive the kick-off, Al Hall, the Rye coach, strolls by. He rolls his eyes at Stanley. Buzz nods: Yes, they're huge, they look well-coached. Later, Buzz says to me: "*I wondered what in hell I'd gotten myself into.*"

Overreaching. Eyes bigger than stomach. Will King be punished for *hubris?* Even the name scares me a little. Which St. Hugh? St. Hugh of Lincoln, the little boy alleged to have been martyred by Jews so that they could use his blood to bake matzoh? No, no. There must be another. No school in New York City would sanction that sort of thing. It's a different St. Hugh. A missionary, maybe.

On the first offensive sequence we're elated by the hard charge of the King line. They're rocketing off the ball, shoving linemen back. Same story. Fieber carries twice: first down. Wilson gets shoved back into his full house backfield. (Something I've never understood about the T-formation. Don't you *lose* blockers with so many men deep, away from the quarterback?) A few runs fail. A pass to Boe is short. Fieber punts.

I'm not functioning well. I'm intoxicated. Clean, cold air, sunlight, trees, old red buildings, the white team and the maroon team, the flashing thighs and taunting knees of the nymphets, the small, congenial crowd. And every now and then I hear someone mention David. "*Watch Green—he destroyed Hamden Hall two weeks in a row."* And I ran from fights. I apologized for insults I never made. I feared "boxing lessons."

On signal from Buzz, David puts King into the basic 5-3. He's the fulcrum again, the nose guard, head to head with a big center. We all look at 78, the gigantic end. He looms over the line of scrimmage like a copper beech in a garden.

Cameron Sillars is having problems. He keeps hitching up his pants. "They're too big," Murray says. "Someone stole his." Cam pulls his trousers up, makes a crashing tackle with his head. Buzz will have to do something about those pants at halftime.

St. Hugh's tries a short, fluttering pass. It isn't much. They don't seem to have a decent passer—no Robinson, no Balasz, no Fasano. Jimmy Wilson catches in on the St. Hugh's forty-five.

On the first play, Fieber takes the pitch and turns the giant's end for twenty yards. The huge boy apparently hasn't got too much foot. He was barely blocked, just moved a little. We're on their twenty-five, what Buzz calls "choke territory." Tacklers try to bring Bobby down, clutch at him, fail. Once more to Fieber. He drags players with him to the twelve. A dump pass to Espo is dropped. Fieber turns left end again, wriggles, spins to the four-yard line under our noses.

And fumbles. St. Hugh's pounces on the ball.

I look in despair at Levison. I dare not look at Norm and Sylvia.

Stanley is raging, striding up and down the sidelines. Iggy stands by for the clipboard. The girls are leading a cheer. No one knows the words.

St. Hugh's goes on the offense. Even though I am wary of underrating opponents, I now have some suspicions about them. They are heavy and menacing. But I suspect they are slow. The secret of prep-school football, I have learned, is *speed*. Rye beat us with two backs who could outrun the King secondary. They weren't a much better team; we annihilated them in the second game. Hamden Hall did it with *one* fast back. They were shoved around mercilessly for two games but won with a few long runs. Deaf did it with the speedy Odom. Were I a prep-school coach,

I'd scout around for a few breakaway runners and get them scholarships. Everything else would fall into line. Passing is negligible
in a high school league; defense can be learned. But fast runners
make the game.

St. Hugh's looks ponderous. On the fifteen they fumble. Andy
Levison rushes past his man, dumps the quarterback. St. Hugh's
recovers, goes into punt formation. There's a bad snap. The kicker
can't handle the ball. It flops around inside the seven-yard line.
Bodies lunge at it, miss it. Greg Anderson, a King sub, recovers
on the four-yard line.

"They've caught it from us," I say to Murray. "It must be the
air."

The team goes into a pro set. It's a 36-power off the veer. David
pulls, leads the blocking. I see him ram his white helmet into the
retreating gut of a linebacker. He blasts the boy, sends him reeling. Fieber prances into the end zone.

We're all on our feet. Is it better because we waited so long? I
cheer, but my cheering is subdued. I live in constant fear of ruin-
ing a good thing, tempting fate, getting my comeuppance.

For the extra points, Dave and Edge pull, lead the blocking
around right end. David drives the giant inside far enough to let
Bobby Fieber go in again. We lead, 8-o.

King kicks off, a long, high boot by Fieber—as good as any that
Fat Charlie got off. St. Hugh's is deep in its own territory. They
can't get untracked. The defense is tough. John Daum, the soccer
goalie, proves to be a rugged defensive end. They can't turn him.
He's an athlete. Edge is having his best game. Dave is spearing,
lunging through the center and the defensive tackles.

I watch David get low—head on the center. He still looks undersized. His move is expertly timed, a swift strong push forward
from the three-point stance. He's in the St. Hugh's backfield.
Their black runner gets stuck for a six-yard loss.

(When we look at the films later, Buzz says: "All I taught them
all year is working now. We should have played a fifteen-game
schedule. We'd have won them all, except maybe Hackley.")

Once more David pierces the St. Hugh's defense. I'll be damned if I know how he does it, low to the ground, his brown face scowling, his heavy thighs pushing like pistons. He slams into the black halfback again. The runner fumbles. Daum recovers.

Fieber is flying. Cam Sillars, stringy, loping, throws a classic block on a linebacker. The field is open for Fieber. He won't stop. Two tacklers try halfheartedly to bring him down. I'm racing to the end zone with him. Norm, Bob's older brother, Jimmy, and Sylvia are dancing alongside, following him. There's a convergence of bodies near the end zone—two St. Hugh's players, Bob —coming together with shuddering force. It looks to us as if he went in. But the referee calls the ball back to the two-yard line. Worse, it is called farther back for holding by Sillars. A typical King disaster. On the sidelines, the Fieber family is raging at the officials. Nobody saw Sillars hold. Everyone thought Bob had scored.

A Boe pass is intercepted. But St. Hugh's can't move against the defense. Andy nails an off-tackle play. No gain. The mysterious Oriental in the St. Hugh's backfield—he's over 200—turns an end, but Mike Mori, half his size, is there to cut him down.

As the quarter ends, we're driving again. Boe makes a superb catch of a Wilson pass and we're on their eleven-yard line. Inexplicably (it's a harbinger of what's to come against Hackley) Buzz goes to the passing game. We know Fieber can destroy them. The blocking is crisp, devastating. Why pass? Boe throws a bad pass to Daum on third down; another incomplete pass on fourth down.

St. Hugh's takes over. Again, David and Andy pile up the play. "You could hear the grunts coming out of them," David tells me that evening.

St. Hugh's manages its longest run of the day—an eleven-yard gain off tackle by the black boy. Wilson intercepts. It's our ball on their forty-six. The half ends. We should be up by three touchdowns. I'll settle for 8-0.

The team looks frustrated as it leaves the field around Buzz.

I can hear his disgusted voice: "You guys will drive me nuts. You should be up by four touchdowns. You get inside the twenty and you fall apart. I want you to destroy them in the second half. I want you to run it up."

Close-the-gates-of-mercy Stanley, like Francis Schmidt at Ohio State. No wonder he worships Bear, reveres Vince's memory. But all coaches have to feel that way. No mercy. Win big. Don't let up. Anyone can be beaten. There is no opponent who, on a given day, cannot be taken.

I want to be alone at halftime. Maybe meditation will win the game for us. Deep down, I know they'll never beat Hackley. Hackley will eat them alive. It's this game or a winless season.

Trying to take solace in David's fine play—jarring tackles, hard blocks—I wander the campus and think back to something Jack Arbolino once told me about a practice session under Lou Little. Enraged at Jack for missing a block, Little grabbed him by the scruff of the neck, shook him, and bellowed in his ear, *"I cannot understand how a human bean cannot know how to block!"*

Arbolino thought a great deal about Lou's comment. How else should a head coach feel? Blocking was like breathing. You were born knowing how to block. There was a center in the brain for blocking. Five-year-old children, grandmothers, Lionel Trilling, all knew how to *block*. It came with the genes. Buzz is like that. His boys were born to block, tackle, run, and *win*. But when? Today?

Another Stanley Special opens the second half. He sends in a secret weapon, a new passer. It is Matt Gormley, a freshman, 5′ 6″, 120 pounds, with a potent arm. They call him "Sonny Jurgensen." Gormley is elfin. Irish, blue-eyed, red-haired. He looks like a born competitor. But I still can't fathom the emphasis on passing, not when Fieber has been devouring yardage, not when the line is blocking so well.

Gormley takes the direct snap, fades, completes a pass. Enough. We go back to basic, meat-and-potatoes football. Fieber running over people, stepping on faces, legs, crotches. Almost without effort, King is on the St. Hugh's sixteen-yard line. It's in the works. A second touchdown.

Murray nudges me. "Bobby goes all the way this time. No sweat."

I believe in nothing any longer. I am the supreme agnostic of football.

They shake Fieber loose inside tackle. He's running without blocks. At the five-yard line all he has to do is race to the corner and he's in. Incredibly, he spins—into the arms of a surprised St. Hugh's defender, who drags him down. The ball pops out of Bob's arms, and St. Hugh's has it on its own five-yard line.

Buzz is screaming. David tries to explain it to me later. "He saw Siganos spin," David says, "and he wants to do the same, only he isn't as fast." It still doesn't explain the fumbling. Nothing does. A superb athlete, intelligent, poised. Is there a genetic code for fumbling, just as Little assumed there was one for blocking? Are human beans inherently structured to fumble or not to fumble?

Tough defense stops St. Hugh's. They can't move an inch. Big Rut embraces the runner, drags him down slowly. Sillars claws his way past blockers, wrestles the same running back to earth. St. Hugh's punts poorly. King has the ball again on the opponents' twenty.

Once again I sniff dread in the air. Oh, the odor is there, along with the Oscar Meyer wieners charring on the grill in back of the swaying stands. It's there, with the Arpège wafting from the tan polo coats of the blonde King mothers, the Canoe floating from the ruddy cheeks of the dads. A November chill tells me I'm aging and full of terrors.

The best hands on the team—Daum. And he drops a touchdown. Why? We pick up yardage, but a penalty moves us back. Third down and fifteen. Murray and I stand foolishly at the sidelines, smiling like dummies, shouting, shivering. I will not give voice to my apprehensions: King needs more than eight points to win. Fieber must score again. Anything. Carry him in.

The lines explode again. Bodies crunching, clacking, grunting. David is thundering toward me. Actually he's after the outside linebacker. He hits him with helmet, shoulders, forearms; blasts him back several yards. Behind David, Fieber is running free. But he cuts too late. He's out of bounds on the two. St. Hugh's takes over on downs.

We say nothing. What is there to say? Is there truly a curse on our sons, something dreadful we did ages ago, some sin for which they are paying the price?

In his anger, Buzz yanks David. He's shouting into his face at the sidelines. I marvel that he can get away with it. Me, I have not raised my voice to my children in five years. They walk away, win arguments, shame me into silence. (They fear only their mother's Latin anger—it erupts about twice a year per child, and it is terrifying. They know mine is counterfeit, formless.)

But there is Stanley grabbing at David's face mask, yanking his brown head back and forth.

"What in hell is wrong with you, Green?" he yells. "Can't you see? When I call for a four-three, I mean a four-three, not a five-three. You lined them up in a five-man front, stupid."

"Okay, so I made a mistake. I didn't see."

Three hundred dollars for contact lenses and he can't see?

"What's two and two, Green?"

"Yeah, yeah, I know."

"Get your ass back in there and play football. Keep your ears open. You people should have scored six times already. You're eating them up but you die inside the twenty."

The third quarter is ending. It's still 8-0. Can they hold on for twelve minutes? Or is there some baroque surprise awaiting us, some unforeseen tragedy? My throat is constricted. My voice is a ragged screech.

The ball is exchanged a few times as the fourth quarter starts. Maybe Fieber is leg-weary. The clouds are closing in. A November frost in the air, icy warnings. If we don't win today, we'll spend a long winter thinking about our misdeeds.

Both teams look exhausted—St. Hugh's from the punishment they've taken, King from frustration and the pain inherent in playing aggressively, "taking it to them." I'm thinking again of spindly Sillars calling Dave at midnight, pondering the reasons for staying with a losing team, absorbing a weekly drubbing. And David, that great guidance counselor, in turn, calling Buzz Stanley, awakening him from a deep sleep at 12:30 A.M. for moral support

They're too close to me. Levison—big, strong, earnest. Rutledge, huge, padded, floating in Fat Charlie's awning of a shirt. Jimmy Wilson; bespectacled Sam Boe; the ineffable Fieber, running forever to the sidelines; square-jawed Eginton, who has played alongside David since sixth grade; LeBlanc, who learned to be a first-rate center in one season; Espo; Daum; gutsy Mori; Barrett . . .

There's an unpleasant lethargy to the game now. The pressure seems to have evaporated. All King has to do is control the ball and the game is theirs. They have shoved St. Hugh's from one end of the field to the other. The New Yorkers have gained about twelve yards through the line for three quarters. There are only a few minutes left.

"Would be nice if they had an extra score," Murray says to me. "Six or eight more points would look good."

He's right. He's worried, just as I am, that some lunatic play, some bolt from above, will turn the game around. All those missed chances, all those lost touchdowns. It's like life, only much worse.

"Pass, pass," everyone shrieks.

Of course, a pass. They can't gain a yard through the stone wall. Buzz knows they'll pass. He's given David the signal for the 4-3 zone. David is playing an outside linebacker position.

The St. Hugh's quarterback eludes the rush. Hands clutch at his shirt. Fear clutches at my bowels.

Years ago I remember reading an interview with a prizefighter who had been knocked out by the young Joe Louis. "You somehow knew when it was coming," he said. "You had a sort of feeling a second before that short left hit you that this was it, and before you knew it, it exploded in your face like a lightbulb."

This is my lightbulb.

The pass is wobbly, high, descending into a crowd. There are at least two St. Hugh's receivers and four King defenders. The dark jerseys look small and inept, because the giant is in their midst. He's bigger than life; he's unnatural.

"Knock it down," we scream.

"Intercept," I croak.

Jimmy Wilson gets a hand on the ball. He tips it. As it moves, not to the ground, but upward and downfield, my heart plunges to my 12-EE Coward arch-supporters. The giant is stumbling, plodding toward the descending ball. With an astonished look on his face, he catches it.

"Oh, Christ," I moan. "The big end."

"He's all alone," Murray cries.

And he is. I can't figure out what happened to the defense. Everyone played the ball. No one stayed deep. Where's Boe? Sillars? Mori? (Mori! I can see that runt trying to bring down this ogre!)

All the lost fights, the double faults, the missed foul shots are rattling around inside my shredded heart. *Not again, please not again.*

The giant is galumphing toward the goal line. The earth trembles under his tread. He isn't fast, but he's huge and terrifying. His enormous stride eats up yardage. The King players are on the ground, or watching, stunned, disbelieving. How? Why? It was a bad pass. The rush was fierce. The receivers were covered. How, in this freakish way in which King School is cursed, did the ball get hit, rise, fall down into the boy's arms?

"He's going," Murray says.

"All the way," Norm says. "That lousy defense."

The giant is gouging divots out of the groomed turf, rumbling over Buzz Stanley's white markers. St. Hugh's bench is hysterical, imploring him to *go all the way.*

Two maroon jerseys are chasing him. It's dark now, appropriately autumnal. Shadows across the green grass. The oaks and maples are black-green. We can barely see which players are chasing the giant.

"It's Mark Barrett," Murray says. "And Dave."

Dimly figured, obscured, little Barrett and David are pursuing the big man. David is hardly the fastest man on the squad. They tried him at fullback once and he couldn't start quickly enough. But there he is, he and Mark, the 135-pound defensive back, shy, unnoticed, pursuing the runner.

"Never get him," Murray says. "He's way ahead."

"Go, Dave!" I shriek. "Go, Mark!"

There are no blockers left. It's the giant against Barrett and Green. The big boy is running along the sidelines. He thunders over midfield, the forty-yard line . . .

At King's thirty-five-yard line, Barrett lunges for his legs. They must be like the pistons on a ship's engine. It's a textbook tackle. Barrett drives all of his 135 pounds into the giant's right leg. Right leg upends. The giant stumbles forward a step, tries to right himself, goes down. He hits the earth like Goliath, Cyclops, a Titan.

We're in the grip of middle-aged hysteria. We pound each other, scream, race down the sidelines, trying to see what's happening.

"The ball's loose," I gasp. "It's loose."

Bouncing erratically, the football comes to life out of the giant's faltering hands. He's in a sitting position, defeated, a fallen angel.

The ball continues its crazy passage, bouncing, popping, doing unnatural things. It moves from the thirty-five to the thirty. David is racing after it. Two St. Hugh's players are running with him. At the twenty-five-yard line, I see David's number 50 fall forward. The blue-and-gold pants also lunge. The ball is downed.

The rest is remembered in a blur—tears, laughter, hugs.

The official is pointing the other way. David has recovered the fumble on his own twenty-five-yard line.

"Penalty," Murray Levison says. "Look."

Beloved referee! He's pacing off fifteen yards against St. Hugh's for a personal foul. One of the St. Hugh's players kicked Dave in the helmet when he went down. The ball is coming back to our forty-yard line. It's all over. The nightmare is ended. We're cheering Barrett and Green as the teams come back. I can't bear to look at the giant. He's stumbling, holding his huge hands out, trying to tell his coach what happened.

"First break of the year," I say to Murray.

"We were due."

It isn't over yet. It never is. Buzz has called a time-out. He wants to make sure nothing goes wrong. All they have to do is play ball control. Rush the ball. Hold on to it. Stick it to them. They're hurting. They blew their big chance. I see the dirty, tense faces of the players. They're congratulating Barrett and David. The game-saving play. The big one. St. Hugh's can't possibly get another break like that.

The girls are leading another long, complicated cheer. I'm so distracted I can't even admire their thighs.

"Go get 'em, King!"

"Two and a half minutes to go."

"One more touchdown, Bobby."

Fieber's off again. He's turned an end, shaken loose on his forty-yard line. He'll go the distance, no question. Levison and I look at one another. Now? Now.

Bobby has daylight ahead. But he spins into the arms of the safety man, whom he drags another ten yards. He misses the touchdown. Yes, he is a true tragic hero—tall, handsome, a bit of the Greek god in him, powerful, swift. Yet he cannot overcome the aimless spins, the awful fumbles. Some malignant demon stalks the great runner. He misses greatness by a hair's breadth; and in his failings, he emerges more enigmatic.

Trembling, I realize that Stanley has started passing again.

Passing? With two minutes to go? "He's a gambler," Murray says. "He knows they're bunched up to stop the run. One good pass and they score. Daum is wide open."

"One good interception and they lose. And the incompletes stop the clock. Don't we want to eat the clock up?"

"Buzz knows what he's doing."

Two trick plays. Gormley trying a bomb. Incomplete. Espo coming around from his wide receiver position, throwing long to Daum. Incomplete. Fieber punts.

St. Hugh's takes over on its own twenty-seven-yard line. The punt coverage is tough. A mob downs the ballcarrier. More grunts. The St. Hugh's players get up slowly. They're bruised, frustrated. But, incredibly, they are down by only eight points. The score should be 48-0, not 8-0.

A pass play—the quarterback is looking for the giant. The ball is thrown short. Sillars intercepts.

"Thirty seconds left," Norm says. "This has to be it. All they have to do is run out the clock. This is the big one."

"Stick 'em, Green," a cheerleader calls.

"Stick 'em, Mean Joe."

"Stick 'em, King."

There's Jimmy Wilson running for the sidelines, out of the wishbone. Why? Why not into the middle of the line? He evidently has missed the handoff to Fieber. And why is he so insistent on going out of bounds and stopping the clock?

At the sidelines, he's tackled. *And fumbles.*

St. Hugh's recovers.

With sixteen seconds left, Stanley calls time again. He's purple with fury. "The season is riding on this," he says. "Dammit, if you blow this one, we scrimmage for an hour after the game. I'll run you around the grounds ten times."

Oh, the bloody unfairness of football! Why can't everybody win, everybody claim a bit of happiness? Why can't we just be enthusiastic, as John Brodie says, and not have to win all the time?

St. Hugh's is lining up. They can do only one thing with sixteen seconds left—throw to the giant. David is back at an outside line-backer position. I wonder what the strategy will be. By now he knows the giant well: 240 pounds. And David at 175. Bump and run? On a man outweighing you by 65 pounds? Who will get bumped?

Screaming fragments my brain. I can't focus. I've abandoned the camera. Who cares about a photo? The enormous end plods downfield. David bumps him, ricochets, the way American infan-trymen used to describe their 90-mm. shells bouncing off German Panzer tanks. Like tennis balls.

The pass is overthrown, batted around, falls to earth.

Seconds left. Who is running the clock? Are we to have a repeat of the U.S.-Russian basketball game in the 1972 Olympics? Is some fiend extending the time and ensuring our defeat?

The scene blurs in front of my fogged eyes. We're under water. Murray, Norm, Jack Rutledge appear in waves and running col-ors. It's damned near nightfall. No sun, no light. And no air for me to breathe. From the knees down, I've liquefied.

"Bump and run on a guy that size," I mutter stupidly.

David's face is black and bloody. He crouches, legs apart, arms ready, waiting for the giant. If they lose, they will deserve to lose. All for nothing. The rebirth of King football—stillborn. The patsies of the Fairchester League. The team that, according to the *Stam-ford Advocate,* loses "laughers." Laugh again, *Advocate.* Laugh at my son and his "hapless" teammates and their "winless" sea-son . . .

Same play, same desperate collision of wills. Coach Valerio must have told his team: "These guys stink. They run up big stats and they fold under pressure. You can beat them with heads-up football."

Levison and LeBlanc are clutching at the quarterback's jersey. How does he stay up? He pulls away, staggers to his right. The arm is back. I shudder for a minute. He has an open field. But I know he's slow. He can't take it all the way.

There are small bursts of automatic fire inside my skull. No voice. No lungs. No heart.

David smashes into the giant again. Last time? Please? The man won't stumble, let alone go down. The script writes itself in my scrambled brain. A last-minute touchdown by St. Hugh's. Two extra points. Someone misses a tackle. We are tied 8-8. A game we should have won seven times.

No one remembers where the ball lands. It's yards away. The giant is grasping at handfuls of cold air. King players are prancing, screaming, hugging one another. It's over. The last play. The quarterback ran too long, used up too much time. Andy and LeBlanc chased him, boxed him in, forced a bad pass.

The official's whistle rings forever in my ears. The clarion of triumph. I see Dave's white helmet tossed high. For the first time this year. They're weeping, laughing, jumping like characters in an animated cartoon.

Andy and Rut and LeBlanc lift Buzz up. They carry him on their shoulders. Someone's trying to sing the King song, but nobody knows the words. Later, I find a copy. It's appropriate. *"Through the years with measured pace, we have learned life's trials to face. Oft we stumbled never fell . . ."* They should change the word to *fumbled*. An unkind thought, and I keep it to myself.

We're like new fathers, Levison, Fieber, Rutledge, Eginton, all of us. We shake hands. Do I detect a fleeting smile on Mr. Boe's face? Is that how he reacts when Dr. J. wins it for the Nets in overtime, or Potvin backhands one past the goalie? It astounds me that this owner of cool professional teams can watch inept King week after week. It is a tribute to his fatherly feelings.

Fond boob that I am, I'm trying to take photographs in the gathering dusk. The scene has turned poignant, mistily sad. Dave is shaking hands with some of his opponents. They're decent kids, good sports. They know they were lucky to come that close. The black boy, the Oriental, the giant. The giant has a confused, apologetic look on his face. I'm staring at his feet. Fourteens? He

pumps Dave's hand. "Nice game, 50." In my crazy way I'm sorry
for him. Susy Martin, the homecoming queen, is getting a bouquet
of flowers. Or is she giving it to someone? I haven't had a drink
in nine years, but now I feel that disengaged buzzing in my head,
the glow of the first martini, the warmth of alcohol.

Susy pays Dave the ultimate tribute. "You were really sticking
today."

No girl ever told me that.

It's dark. The St. Hugh's players are boarding their bus. They'll
get another chance next year. Joe Valerio is talking to Buzz.
Coaches' talk. They get along. I want to run to the bus and say
to them: "Look, you guys played well. You were up against a
better team. You weren't disgraced."

"You won't believe the stats," I hear one of the assistant coaches
say to Norm Fieber. "We had twenty-seven first downs and they
had four. We gained over three hundred yards and they gained
seventy-nine, most of which was on that long pass. How in heck
did we win by only eight points?"

I'll settle for it. I'll take it, thank you. All favors accepted.

King players drift off to the locker room. I shake David's hand,
try to get a few photos of him. "For God's sake, Dad, will you
please cut it out?" He is embarrassed by my affection. I understand too well. I never could abide it when my own father hud-
dled around me, fussed, tried to take my photograph. What's so
great about me? Our children treasure their privacy. They want
to be anonymous, unparented.

I recall Dave and Ted learning to roller skate in Paris, outside
our apartment on the Champs de Mars. After a few minutes
they'd trudge upstairs and refuse to go out again. "Why? Why
are you back?" Marie would ask. The answer was a volume: *The
French are staring at us.*" It was true. All France was staring at
them. And they deserved to be stared at in their New York Mets
jackets and jeans, with their American voices. Don't stare at me;
don't tread on me; don't call me MF.

In the locker room, frenzy. John Daum's birthday cake is hurled against the lockers. Gatorade is poured on sweaty heads. There are shrieks, curses, towels snapped on naked butts. They're looking ahead. "Kill Hackley," someone says. "Destroy Hackley," they cry. If St. Hugh's can be devastated, why not Hackley next week?

When I hear about this later, from David, both of us basking in the glow of the victory, reliving that darkening sky, the cheering crowd, the homecoming queen, I shiver slightly. For God's sake, I want to warn him, don't tempt the fates. Hackley may have lost every game, but they are big-time and tough, a team that almost beat St. Luke's. What if someone snitches to their coach? "Those smart-ass kids from King," I can hear the spy saying, "they're hollering 'Kill Hackley.' " They'll remember. They'll be waiting.

At our cars, Murray Levison shakes my hand. "They did it, tiger."

"They were terrific. They should have won four games, maybe five. They murdered Rye the second time. And those two games with Hamden Hall. They had them won."

"But they won at least one. I'd hate to see the kids end up without a single win. It hurts a long time."

In semidarkness, under the garage light, David and I are shooting baskets. I'm too old to go one-on-one. My paunch droops, and for a man who doesn't smoke or drink, my wind is despairingly short. A few drives to the basket and I'm wheezing.

But I can still sink fouls. I feel I have to buoy him with some marginal athletic skill. I drop twelve in a row, choke, hit the front rim. The best he can do is six.

"We had a pretty good team in the old 827th Ordnance," I tell him. "We were runner-ups for the depot championship. Almost made the All-England finals."

"Stupid two-handed set shots."

"What's wrong with them?" *Swish.* A perfect arc. The ball drops delicately into the net. The cords rise, whistling.

"You'd be rejected every time. They'd give you a Spalding sand-
wich as soon as you let the ball go."

"Spal—?"

"What Bill Russell calls it. When you slam the shot into the
shooter."

He takes over, popping long, arching one-handed bombs from
across the driveway. Buzz wants him to help flesh out the basketball team. No way, David says. He knows he isn't good enough,
and he likes hockey better than anything. Better than football,
tennis, skiing. Hockey is all. He and his friend John Hanley are
in a league in Ridgefield. Ice time is more precious in Fairfield
County than a 44-foot Wagner pool, rare than a Button Gwinnett
signature. Teams have been known to play at four in the morning.

I start telling him about a basketball game we played in England thirty years ago. Quarter-finals. A trip by truck at night
from our depot at Tewkesbury to Bristol, to play an Army hospital team. The road became fogged in a thick yellow mist. We had
to take turns walking in front of the truck with a flashlight, leading the six-by-six at five miles an hour half the way to Bristol. We
got there at one in the morning. Incredibly, our opponents were
waiting for us. Our coach, a junior high school athletic director,
Corporal Ohmsted, had phoned ahead.

I describe the dimly lit gym. It was freezing. Our teeth chat-
tered as we took our warm-ups. We had blue-and-gold uniforms,
with "827" on the shirts. The team had no height but it was fast
and everyone could shoot. We had one genuine athlete—a sergeant named Murphy who had played freshman basketball in
New Mexico. He had one of the first one-handed set shots I ever
saw outside of the famed Stanford team of 1939 that played City
College in Madison Square Garden. In the era before contact
lenses, Murphy wore a heavy face mask over his eyeglasses. He
was nearsighted, but he moved well. The rest of us were schoolyard basketball players. I particularly recall our 6′ 2″ center.
His name was Walmark, a boy from Williamsburg, Brooklyn,
an apprentice baker, who had enjoyed a brief career as a light-

heavyweight. I don't know why, but we called him Hymie, although his name was Earl.

"You won?" David asks. It's dark now. We are shooting baskets in the chill night, trying to reaffirm some old bond. Like primitive man sitting around a wood fire, boasting of famous hunts. It's a bit like a Jack London novel. Our retriever, Caesar, squats over his hoard of old tennis balls. He's part of it. The law of club and fang.

"Yes. Low-scoring game. Something like 25-22. They were a tall team but sloppy. I played most of the second half."

"You score?"

"A few buckets." Then it comes back to me. Lost moments of heroism, of rising above my meager speed and marginal talent. "Ohmsted sent me in to guard a guy with a big reputation. I think he wanted me to foul him, get him into a fight. He was a big, strong Slav of some kind, made the All–Southern England team. Podanik, or Podolnik, something like that. Rugged, blond, huge shoulders. He had a lot of fancy moves with his head and shoulders. And he had that funny habit of holding the ball over his head with two hands before passing it, feinting passes, flexing his wrists. Like this."

I take the ball and demonstrate. "The master at this was a player named Dutch Garfinkel of St. John's. But only Garfinkel could get away with it. I had the feeling that Podavnik was all form. That he didn't know what he was doing with the ball or anything else."

"Come on, Dad. You took a big guy like that?"

"I'd learned tough defense at the Brooklyn Jewish Center from the great Sammy Schoenfeld. Twice, while he was making those fancy overhead moves with the ball, I batted it out of his hands, ran behind him, and went all the way for the lay-up. There was hardly anyone in the stands at one in the morning but I got a hand. It took us three hours to get back to camp. The fog was general throughout England."

"But you weren't really great?"

"No, son. Just a sub. But I helped out. The depot champs killed us. They were too good. They had two men who were All–Pacific Coast Conference, and a lieutenant who was six foot eight."

The story is a form of tribute on my part. Marie's right. He's suffered bruises, exhaustion, tears, humiliation, failure all year. But who can doubt that in part he did it to compensate for my daily migraine, my sloth, my slovenly backhand? I owe him something. Of course the debt, like all such debts, will never be paid. Odd, how I've been caught in the middle. I owed my father too much too. The bill was barely honored; not that he cared. And now I have the sensation that my children have done far more for me than I can ever do for them. Is this a failing on my part, or is it the nature of the nuclear family? Maybe the primitives with their extended families, the uncles and aunts who function as quasi-parents, have a better notion—maybe these numerous relationships reduce guilt, increase the small acts of politeness and support that make life bearable.

Andy Levison pulls into the driveway. They're off to the blast to end all blasts. At Rutledge's, of course. Coach Stanley will be there, and the assistants, and all the Lolitas.

Silent on a peak near Darien, I watch the car wind down the road. Next year I'll have to hire someone to pick up David's workload. I can't even get the lawnmower to run. I fear the spreader. I'm like an Arab or a Zulu who wants to raise a mob of sons so that some of them will take care of him in his old age. The house will have to go. Goodbye to Green's Hill.

"Did you ask him about his head?" Marie asks, as I enter.

"His head?"

"You said he got kicked. Didn't the other team get a penalty when they kicked Dave in the helmet?"

"Yes, he did get kicked." Foul father! I've forgotten. I didn't even ask him after the game. No one did. It couldn't have been much of a kick. Enough for the penalty, of course. But in the frenzy, the joy of that dusky afternoon, who cared about David's head? "Ah, he seems fine. No pain, nothing. Not like after St. Luke's with the frozen jaw. He ate tonight, didn't he?"

"Very little. He was overstimulated."

"You sound like my mother. I was always being overstimulated and forced to go to bed early, when I was actually lethargic and understimulated. I wish now and then I could really be overstimulated. But I guess it's too late."

In the basement I inspect the Cathedral of Bitonto. He's done a pretty good job. With colored markers he's inked in the arcades and chapels in the side walls. The rose window needs a bit more color, and the columns outside the portals, while well drawn, seem to rest on lizards instead of lions. The eagle over the arched doorway droops a little. But no matter. The Norman cathedral is taking form.

I must tread carefully in the basement. David and John Hanley have dismantled an old Ping-Pong table and set the halves up at opposite ends of the basement as hockey goals. The floor is littered with gloves, sticks, pucks, padding. A foot in both worlds, I tell myself. The mind must be kept open, and the body strong.

Marie asks if I want to watch television with her; there's a discussion program on PBS that might interest me. Normally I would. But not the night after the St. Hugh's game.

"No, I'll read. Something light and aimless, so I can think about the way they tackled the giant."

10

Like a chronic boozer who hides bottles in secret cupboards, I stow bits and pieces of the St. Hugh's game in the corners of my mind. It will sustain me for a long time. Depressed, in the iron grip of migraine, breathless and inept when I try to return a hard serve, I will buoy myself up with memories of that famous victory.

Admittedly, that 8-0 triumph is a small part of the action, but it will do me fine. All those losses make the solitary win more dazzling. And who knows? Maybe Buzz Stanley will pull the upset of upsets and knock off Hackley next Saturday.

A final victory would give King a 2-5-1 season. Good, good. When I play tennis, I'm satisfied if I win a set. Preferably the first set. Having claimed my widow's mite, I can hit out, relax, lose generously. A poor thing but my own. Dink shots, soft lobs, corners and alleys. Let them make the errors.

Am I out of step with the times and the standards? Probably. "I am jealous of everyone else's success," Frank Yablans, the film executive, is quoted as saying. "I want it all." My problem—or is it a virtue?—is that I don't really "want it all." Just something to stroke now and then, like Lennie's dead mouse. Well, now I have it. Oh, I can be driven into a fit of jealous sulks when an unworthy novelist gets a rave front-page notice in the *Times Book Review,* thanks to his connections and friends. Marie says that writers, next to film directors, are the world's most envious people. Okay, I accept the stigma. But that still doesn't mean I "want it all." I'll settle for a plot of earth, not the whole staked plain.

Joseph Wood Krutch tells about a restaurant banquet he attended given by Thomas Wolfe after Wolfe had gotten a royalty check. The gargantuan Wolfe, craving everything in excess, kept ordering vast quantities of food and drink, to the distress of his guests, most of them intellectuals like Krutch. "I want more," Thomas Wolfe commanded. "More lobster. More champagne. More music. More women." At this point, Ben Gitlow, a small, frazzled, aging leftist, turned to Krutch and muttered: "I wish Tom would understand that, in my own small way, I'm every bit as Rabelaisian as he is."

Are we Americans Wolfes or Gitlows? Certainly our national leaders in politics, business, and the arts seem to be heavily weighted on the Wolfean side. Richard Nixon didn't want merely to win elections; he wanted to obliterate everyone who ever sneered at him. Kick asses, he told John Dean, this is a war. "I wouldn't want to be on the other side right now," our President said.

Once I mentioned film director X to film director Y, allowing as how I thought X had done a rather good job on his last film. Y's eyes narrowed and he halted my laudatory comments with a raised palm. "X is a man of microscopic talent and less taste." End of discussion. How we love to eat each other alive, like praying mantises in a terrarium. It is said that the day after Arthur Miller's *Death of a Salesman* opened to ecstatic notices, the wife of another playwright developed a headache that lasted for a year. Too many of us have become little Yablanses, crowing at the other fellow's box office disaster, gloating over our own big score.

Maybe the jocks are not as bad as the others. Red Smith pointed out that, while Vince Lombardi made a religion out of winning, he never won dishonestly, never sanctioned dirty football, and never failed to praise his opponents—win or lose. The observation makes Lombardi more palatable to me (who can explain the intense national mourning over his death, the hysterical worship?), but I remain concerned about his single-mindedness. It was victory—or *nothing*. Could he have really felt that way? No one mentions that after he left Green Bay he lost games in Washington.

John Brodie, the former quarterback for the San Francisco Forty-Niners, points out that the way professional football is set up, there are twenty-five losers every year and only one winner. The winning team is a "bunch of gloating, self-satisfied hot-shots." There are twenty-five other groups of players who feel inadequate, frustrated, and second-rate. He argues that professional golf is a far saner and healthier sport. The pros take turns; everyone gets a nibble at glory, some a big bite, some a taste. But no one really loses. Golfers, he says, are relatively free of the compulsion to win at all costs. In pro football, he argues, the standard of judgment should be *enthusiasm:* whether the players did their best, the extent to which they tried hard, wanted to win. No shame should attach to losing a game or coming in second. All pro football players, Brodie concludes, are winners. (The *Times,* running this excerpt from Brodie's book, got the sense of the piece all wrong, in the headline, which read, *"You Play to Win, But if You Are Not Enthusiastic, You May Lose."* That is not at all what the piece is about. But evidently the national mania over winning infects even *Times* deskmen.)

Brodie's right. For years fans and sportswriters have criticized Tom Landry and the Dallas Cowboys and John Madden's Oakland Raiders because "they don't win the big ones." What nonsense! Landry and Madden may not be charmers, and I feel rather strange rushing to their defense. But over the years they have won many more games than they have lost. What is this preoccupation with "big ones"? Is it possible that the Cowboys and the Raiders get beaten by better teams, that they do their level best and lose naturally, without any hint of faintheartedness or choking?

Some years ago the New York Yankees were rumored to have

fired Yogi Berra as manager because he failed to win the World
Series. *Failed to win the World Series!* Ye gods and little children!
He won the pennant in the American League, didn't he? What
did they want from the poor man? Again, the obsession with *absolute* victory, total domination, gobbling everything in sight,
must have been at work. The Yankee owners *wanted it all.*

Inevitably for a writer such musings must lead to Norman
Mailer. Here is the Frank Yablans, the Richard Nixon, the Vince
Lombardi of novelists. He is the King Charles Head of American
literature, inescapable, inevitable, everywhere at once. There
seem to be four of him. Yes, yes, he's brilliant, talented, our only
resident genius. *You tell it, darling,* as the song goes. No two people have ever been so in love—Mailer the performing self and
Mailer the writer. None of this is really bad, except for the contempt with which he treats his peers. Reading *Armies of the
Night* (of course, it's brilliant, insightful, marvelously written)
we get Mailer's judgments on defenseless naïfs like Paul Good-
man, Martin Luther King, Dwight MacDonald, and Nelson Algren. Nothing is to be gained by repeating the abuse. Maybe it's
embarrassing even to Mailer by now. But there it is. And why?
Well, they're *competition.* They may grab some of the spotlight at
the meetings and marches. Knock 'em off!

All this, of course, is mere prelude for what Mailer has in store
for Arthur Miller in *Marilyn.* What did Miller ever do to him to
merit such a pounding? He did plenty, just by being Miller—a
good playwright, maybe even a better playwright than Mailer is
a novelist. Worse, he gets a fair amount of publicity. Worst of all,
he possessed the national Venus, knew her, explored her, loved
her. Mailer did not. After him! Destroy him! How dare he get to
the national sex goddess before the great existentialist! It is all so
patent, so obvious, so little-boyish that one wonders sometimes
about the true impulses.

Ah, but this is a lighthearted book about a game played by
boys. Still, I cannot help but shiver when I think about this obsession of ours with winning all, crushing enemies, rising ever to

the top. We are discovering, these gray days, that we cannot knock down all the trees, pump all the oil, corner all the gold, grow all the wheat. We cannot even win all the wars. I hope we will not become hysterical children, tantrum-ridden and violent in our frustration. If the ubiquitous man-in-the-street Americans *en masse* are nothing more than a mob of little Mailers or Yablanses or Nixons, then we are in for a sterner testing than the mild knocks we are now experiencing. Gluttons and monomaniacs come to bad ends. Maybe we must learn to settle for less, be gracious about it, adopt more of the golfer's mentality than the football coach's.

Fat chance. On the very day on which I write these words, the sports page of the *New York Times* fills me with a morbid sense of being out of step. Two national leaders, President Ford and Woody Hayes, slap me down:

FORD STRESSES WINNING
AS AMERICAN TRADITION

Speaking to the National Football Foundation, the President asserts that when he played for Michigan, he played "to win, not to get exercise, gold or glory, but simply to win." Mr. Ford went on: "To me winning is not a shameful concept. I like to think that winning is in the American tradition."

A few picky observations: What about the fact that one of Mr. Ford's teams lost seven out of eight of its games? And when has anyone with a smidgin of sense—or anyone at all—regarded winning as "shameful"? Does anyone go out *wanting* to lose? The President, and many like him, protests too much. Such a *geshrei* is raised about winning that one suspects what may lie behind it —a neurotic fear of losing and a determination to win *no matter how*. Ends and means again.

Coach Hayes makes it even more explicit. As reported by Red Smith, Hayes says: "I don't think it's possible to be too intent on winning . . . this country is built on winning and winning alone."

In the course of his press conference, this molder of men then lets it all hang out. The Watergate coverup? "I would have done the same thing," Coach Hayes says, "and I consider myself an honorable man." Naturally, if winning is everything, the only thing, if the country is built on winning *alone*, it must follow that one must do anything in one's power—provided that one doesn't get caught!—to win. Presumably that includes a president, intent on winning an election, who lies, subverts the Constitution, commits crimes, undermines the structure of the two-party system, and brings disgrace to his office. He wanted to win, didn't he?

If winning is the only thing, we are allowed to do anything to win. Isn't that what it's all about? Thank God, say I, for referees, judges, and the press.

President Ford would probably be the first to add a footnote to his speech. We want to win, of course, but we should win honorably, fairly, graciously. But surely he and others like him should realize that a national monomania based on beating the other guy —harmless in itself—can only lead to Nixonian and Hayesian perversions of life itself?

Oh, these obsessed winners, these ferocious, never-say-die coaches, team owners, presidents. Something doesn't quite mesh as I think of them. There's a gear slipped, an eccentric wheel not functioning. During the pro football playoffs, it dawns on me what's wrong. Amid much fanfare, it is disclosed that Rocky Bleier, the running back of the Pittsburgh Steelers, is the *only professional football player to have served in Vietnam*. No slight is intended here against Mr. Bleier, who was wounded, decorated, told he could never play football again, pleaded for a try-out and matured into a star. (He is also a graduate of my old Brooklyn high school, Samuel Jones Tilden.)

But the *only* pro football player to make it to Vietnam? Amid all those thousands and thousands of hearty, able, rugged, combative physical specimens? One wonders. Either this fierce drive to win, this compulsion to cast aside everything in life except absolute victory, is not quite as bone-deep among our jocks and jock-supervisors as we have been led to believe. Or—and perhaps this is closer to the truth and I am being mean-spirited—the agony and bloodiness and pointlessness of Vietnam were never popular even among our most winning-prone young citizens.

Yes, winning is everything, winning is all that matters. And if fielding a winning football team means perhaps losing a war, so be it. What irony! Deep down in their athletic hearts, the coaches and owners and general managers were reluctant radicals, closet counterculturists, premature peaceniks. Look at their record in sending their finest flower to crush Hanoi and keep Ho Chi Minh from invading Hawaii. Is it possible that under the skin hippie and jock are the same person?

Fully realizing the hopelessness of my position, I raise a small, shy voice to ask, is winning *really* the only thing, everything, that which makes us great, strong, powerful, envied? Might there conceivably be other values, other goals? What about compassion, generosity, affection, humor, the intellect, the arts? Yes, we have winners in science and architecture and sculpture, and some humanitarians save more lives than others. But I suspect that these people who move society along, save lives, build cities, create beautiful works, do not conceive of their skills as "winning"—and certainly not at any price.

Jonas Salk and Albert Sabin were bitter rivals, but when Salk's polio vaccine was accepted first for national use, I doubt that the public conceived of Sabin as a "loser." Some years later, Sabin's oral vaccine replaced Salk's vaccine. Was he then the "winner"? History will judge both men as great scientists, benefactors, men of intellect and dedication who did much to alleviate human suffering. The millions of children spared the agonies of infantile paralysis will never be concerned over which scientist "won" and which "lost." Mankind can be proud of both men.

End of moralizing. I'll keep watching football a long time, fascinated by the speed and the timing—and the violence. In a sense, the spectator, especially the TV viewer, gets a limited view of what's going on. It took books like Gary Shaw's *Meat on the Hoof,* or Dan Jenkins's *Semi-Tough*, or Pete Gent's *North Dallas Forty* to make me appreciate the blood and bruises involved in the game. We see only midgets in funny round hats and wide shoulders and tight knickers dancing around. Occasionally one is injured, twitches, writhes, is carried off. But we are spared the true agonies. Maybe that's why Don Meredith and Frank Gifford always seemed to evince a faint contempt for Howard Cosell. Combat troops sneering at a rear-echelon clerk. He was not one of them, had never tasted dirt, sucked in his own blood, felt the cartilege snap, the bone break. Still, it's as good a way as any to waste a Sunday afternoon, and if my son is now part of the great national confraternity of helmeted jocks, I'm happy. He has become one of Lou Little's "human beans," born knowing how to block.

The first Monday in November finds me reading the *Advocate* with shimmering joy. The headline is a tonic, a bracing breeze,

KING TASTES VICTORY
ZIPS ST. HUGH'S, 8-0

Bob Fieber scored a first quarter touchdown and the King defense limited St. Hugh's to only 83 yards' total offense as the Vikings won their first contest of the season, 8-0, Saturday, in Stamford.

Fieber, who gained 124 yards in 24 carries, had runs of 45 and 32 yards nullified by penalties. . . .

King's defense completely dominated the 1-6-0 New Yorkers, forcing seven turnovers. Jim Wilson swiped a pair of tosses and Mark Barrett had another. Dave Green turned in the defensive play of the game when he recovered a fumble jarred loose by Barrett after St. Hugh's had completed a 60-yard pass. . . . "Now that we've won," said Coach Buzz Stanley, "we have a chance to upset Hackley."

Tempting fate again, the Buzzer. The article tells me something I don't want to be reminded of: Hackley, although 0-7, is good. They were leading St. Luke's in the fourth quarter but lost 18-6 on some last-minute heroics by Mike Siganos.

Dave comes home from school. He's been selected athlete of the week for the second time. There was praise from Joe Valerio, the St. Hugh's coach. Dave shows me a maroon strip of cloth, about three inches wide and a foot long. On it, embroidered in script, is the legend: BEAT HACKLEY.

"Something for the cheerleaders?" I ask.

"Nope. Buzz wants them sewn on the backs of our shirts. We're going to stick it to them."

"But . . . taunting them like that? Maybe it will get them mad."

"Buzz says we have to psych them out from the start."

"They almost beat St. Luke's. It says so here." I show him the article. He's pleased. They're no longer "winless, hapless" King.

"Yeah. They have this guy Guzzo, the toughest lineman in the league. He got Balasz, St. Luke's quarterback, thrown out. Siganos ran back an interception eighty yards."

Change of jockstraps; there's hockey tonight. A pick-up game with some older boys, some men. There's barely time to eat, rub his wounds. I hear him upstairs laboring into his hockey padding. The goalie's mask intrigues me. It was originally white, but he's painted it red and blue, in Navajo geometrics. I ask for and get a short course in the differences between jockstraps, or if you will, cups. The hockey apparatus is a true cup, green, plastic, hard. The football protector is a hard elastic.

"Ever hear of Foul-proof Taylor?" I ask.

"Nope."

In the small room adjacent to his cluttered bedroom, Marie is reluctantly sewing the BEAT HACKLEY legend onto old number 51. The team will go back to its white jerseys for the last game. Hackley wears black, the color of death.

"Taylor was the man who invented the protective cup. For catchers, I believe. He used to go around wearing this metal cup under his trousers and ask baseball players to belt him in the crotch with a bat. They did. And he stood tall. He never felt a thing. That's how the cup for catchers was adopted. Before that they had lots of injuries. A bit of baseball history."

"Sounds crazy."

And he's gone, lugging an L. L. Bean duffle bag full of his goalie impedimenta.

For some reason, as I watch him shoulder his way through the door, rugged, potent, heedless of contact and pain, I am still thinking of Norman Mailer. Something he wrote once. Something about watching his sons grow up to be . . . football players? I rummage through the paperbacks in my library and find the passage in *The Armies of the Night*.

Mitten der innen Mailer injects a soliloquy on his sons as potential athletes in a passage about getting jailed in Washington with other antiwar demonstrators. (It is a brilliant passage. Mailer manages to make his two nights in a Washington jail sound like four years in Buchenwald. We weep for his wrinkled suit, his difficulty in calling his wife, the prolonged absence from his family. Magician that he is, he convinces us he has truly *suffered*.)

I reread the paragraph, and I realize I have reached some turning point in my life, a watershed.

Perhaps because of his sons, he saw everything in terms of football these days; he could see each of his boys in twenty years on a professional football team. The older one was wild and fierce and angelic and delicate, graceful as a young prince, sly as a thief—he would make a great running back, a superb pass receiver. He was competitive as a maniac when he wanted to win. The younger one was capable of taking tremendous punishment (at present from his older brother). He was going to play linebacker, no doubt (and with his sleeves rolled up). He would be enormous, and very powerful, and with the happiest disposition in the world, for his brain was keen, his eye quick.

Und so weiter. Harmless dreams for a man with small boys. Identical with some of my own fantasies and those of millions of Americans, including my new friend Mr. O'Dowd. Football is, after all, the national religion, our *Bushido*, the moral and physical code under which you are tested.

And now, sweet moment of revelation, I understood that at long last I had an edge on Mailer. Whether we like his writing or not, he is the yardstick by which every American writer measures himself. I don't mean one's work, but rather one's public image, one's power to manipulate the media, to make the system work for the writer rather than permitting it to subdue or, worse, ignore him. Sooner or later every American scribbler ends up at Mailer's door, peeking through the keyhole, sifting his garbage, either worshiping at his shrine or burning him in effigy. The man has contrived this masterfully. While some of us may be repelled by his egomania, his sly advocacy of violence—I didn't really mean it, he pleads—and his cunning ambivalence over political and social issues, we cannot avoid him. Indeed, how can one avoid a man who, writing about the Chicago riots of '68, excuses his absence from a head-busting foray on the ground that he had a previous invitation to Hugh Hefner's party? And does this *seriously*, and gets the important critics and reviewers to nod their heads and agree with him. (Did Trotsky get his start this way? By sipping vodka with the Yusupoffs and Troubetzkoys? Mailer's problem is that he is the only revolutionary who is also a beautiful person. He is half Bela Kun, half Suzy Parker.)

Oh, there's also the *macho*, the muscle-flexing, the adolescent bragging about how much he gets, the sneering at lesser orders, the proclamations of great deeds. Now, in *The Armies of the Night*, I dig out another Mailerian ego trip: He wills his sons to be great football players. (Knowing his capacity for fulfilling his own prophecies, I have the uneasy feeling that his sons will indeed end up with the Jets or Giants.) But that's Christmas Future. For the moment, the edge is here, on Green's Hill, in suburban Stamford. Maybe ten years from now *Time* will run pictures of Mailer's halfback and linebacker sons. For the moment I have climbed the mountain first, I have watched the blood of my blood throw hard, jolting blocks, crash into runners, read the offense, chase the quarterback, stick and get stuck. I have seen him crack his palm against an opponent's helmet, fire off the three-point stance, blow the man out, plunge into the thicket of organized violence, and get to his feet, bloodied, dirtied, happy. My son also rises.

Marie finds me chuckling as I read *The Armies of the Night.* Why? she asks.

"I'm one up on Mailer. He's dreaming of his sons' becoming football players. Mine has."

"You're wildly jealous of him."

"Isn't everybody?"

I show her the story in the *Advocate.* Dave Green, the man who saved the game with a recovered fumble. She suggests I sweep the garage. Sleepwalking, I hustle garbage cans and rakes to the driveway. Mailerisms skitter through my head.

There was dread in the lawnmower and cancer in the seed spreader. It was apparent to Green that the devil had at last won, displacing God from the leaky sacks of fertilizer, possessing the extension ladder, poisoning the mulch. The push brooms stank of vomit, and the plastic vapors given off by the trowels and rakes conjured up nightmares of death and mutilation that danced crazily in his brain.

Hefting bags of turf builder and lime, I decide that the American writer's pursuit of *macho*, his display of fists and genitalia, is more laughable than noxious. Poor fellow! He sits hunched over his typewriter day after day. Thighs enlarge, eyes fail to focus. Worst of all he lives with the knowledge that the Middle American masses regard him as odd, queer, a sissy, a freak. What to do? *Why, of course!* Cock the right, jab with the left. Curse, kill birds and animals, boast about beaten opponents, seduced women, the big money.

"I'll get you in a dark alley," Mailer is said to have muttered to Alan Lelchuk, a young writer, who treated him uncivilly in a novel. George Frazier reports that John Steinbeck kept bragging about how he had "killed a man with my own hands." And the model for all: Ernest Hemingway. He laughed as he shot hyenas in the gut, applauded as, insane with pain, they ate their intestines. At least he came by it honestly. His ancestors probably shot

Indians. In Mailer's case it is less comprehensible. Harvard, Brooklyn, Jewish, New York. All this must be overcome. America, which he sees so full of dread, cancer and vomit, must accept him on its own terms. (It won't work, Norman. I saw a documentary film in which a group of Archie Bunkers sat in a bar in Queens and watched Mailer perform on television. The consensus about Aquarius: "He's a Communist.")

The braggarts, the cocksmen, the big winners are all in step with the new mythologizers, the Ardreys and the Lorenzes, who would have us believe in that wicked ancestor ape-man, bashing his neighbor with a pointed stick and lunching on his brains. Yes, we know about man's inherent brutality, how he defends his food, his turf, his women. And maybe we are worse than wolves and African Kobs and sticklebacks. (So much has been written about these battling fish that I have a feeling they're fakes, wind-up toys kept by a nut scientist who rents them out to biological popularizers. Besides, a stickleback sounds to me like a free safety who likes to tackle hard.)

Joseph Wood Krutch, toward the end of his life, probably felt as pessimistic as Lorenz and the others who had made deductions about human behavior from close observation of the ruffed grouse and the Canadian goose. But Krutch did concede that they underrated environment. Colin Turnbull's horrible Africans, the Ik, who cheated, lied, stole, and defecated on one another's doorsteps, were driven to this behavior by loss of their hunting lands, destruction of their food supply, and the very real threat of extinction. The Tasaday people of the Philippines, in marked contrast, are gentle, polite, and unwarlike. They have never suffered a lack of food and have never been threatened by outsiders. Even a firm believer in Original Sin and the Basic Rottenness of Man would have to concede that under stress and deprivation, people behave worse than when they are eating regularly.

Nonetheless, Krutch maintained that man was basically a destroyer determined to use up the earth, kill anything that moved.

"*Some* men, Joe," I argued. "And maybe in different degrees. Humanitarians didn't build Auschwitz, we know, and too many civilized Europeans applauded places like Auschwitz. But a few . . ."

I told him about an incident when David was seven years old. He had caught a trout in the river that runs at the bottom of our hill. It was alive and wiggling when he brought it up that evening. He decided to put it in a pail of fresh water. The next morning he would eat it for breakfast. In the morning I found him standing over the wiggly fish with a knife, looking at it for all the world like Abraham studying the trussed figure of Isaac. Feeling not unlike the angel of the Lord, I asked him what he intended to do.

"Dad," he said. "I can't kill this fish." He put it in the pail, trudged down the hill and returned it to the stream. I suspect many parents have witnessed similar scenes. Arthur Godfrey wept after he killed his first elephant and decided he could never do it again. So I have the feeling that the urge to murder, to destroy, to annihilate is not quite so strong as Messrs. Ardrey, Lorenz, Tiger, and Morris insist it is. (I liked Desmond Morris better when he was explaining how women's breasts evolved into their adorable roundness in imitation of buttocks. *That*, I feel, is damned good science.)

Perhaps football serves its purpose and serves it well. Men get hurt, but few die. It's violence, but it is orderly, orchestrated. To see one's own flesh and blood in the middle of this storm of arms and legs, to know he is participating bravely and well, maybe that is a civilized and acceptable level of injury. I went duck hunting once in my life and I grieved over those dead greenheaded mallards for days. Limit the violence I must observe and condone, and I'll happily surrender all rights to it—to any writer, any quasi-scientist who feels he needs an extra measure of murder. Besides, what do they know about Buzz Stanley's 6-2 defense, gapping the guards with the tackles wide?

I'm still looking for excuses not to go to the Hackley game. For all the brave reports from practice, I am filled with shivering doubts. David has painted his shoes white for the event—or ordeal. There are *extra* American flags on the helmets. The taunting BEAT HACKLEY has been sewn to every white jersey. I wonder whether Hackley can be psyched. They're a hungry team, an enraged team, 0-7 against a schedule of monsters. The boys will be like pythons deliberately starved for a medical experiment. A rabbit will be dropped into the cage. A white rabbit with an American flag on its forehead.

"We're invited to Boston University for the weekend," Marie announces.

She explains. The Boston University Library, to which I've donated my manuscripts, is having a banquet to celebrate its one-millionth book. I'm a guest of honor. (A last-minute one, I suspect, but no matter.) They're honoring Rex Harrison, who has given them his papers too.

"But what about our nose guard?"

"Your nose guard."

"That's right. I never promised you a nose guard."

"You keep that up," Marie says, "and I'll go up there alone and run off with Rex Harrison."

I ignore her. "Try this. 'Where it will all end, nose guard.' "

"Worse."

"Dave says they can win it—go out in a blaze of glory."

"No. Enough of that lunacy. Watching him get beaten up every week. And the way the coach yells at him! You said you were shocked."

"Someone's got to yell at him. It doesn't bother the kid."

"I'm sending a telegram to Dr. Gotlieb at Boston University. We're going to the banquet."

My protests grow feebler. I'm glad to be off the hook. It's like the scary part of a movie when I was a little boy. Close my eyes and it will be all over. I won't watch another massacre of the innocents. I know too much about Hackley. They are so dirty, so foul-mouthed they frighten even opposing coaches. The indomitable Dick Whitcomb of St. Luke's, the team of Siganos, Smith, Fat Charlie, Oldford, was appalled by them. How will little King respond? Will Mike Mori take them on? Mark Barrett? Dave?

(I have a blinding memory of a game between Columbia and Michigan at Baker Field during my undergraduate years in the early 'forties. Yes, Michigan. Lou Little feared no one. His 175-pound linemen played sixty minutes. They beat Georgia one year, Wisconsin the next. But Michigan was too powerful. It was four deep. At one point, leading by three touchdowns, Michigan sent in an *entire new team*. Unfazed, Little countered by sending in a new halfback, a friend of mine named Phil Bayer, 160 pounds. "They send in a *team*," Mel Hershkowitz said sadly, "we send in Bayer." Hackley, I fear, will be King's Michigan.)

David is not upset that I will miss the Hackley game. He will be cool in his white shoes, BEAT HACKLEY sticker, new flag. "We're going to beat them, Buzz says," he tells me the day before the game. "Buzz says they play a tough four-four defense, big tackles. He says if we can run right at their strength, send Fieber off tackle, we can dominate them."

I wish him well. As we pack the car for the Boston trip, more tidbits: A Hackley lineman told the headmaster of St. Luke's to "go fuck." The Hackley players regard opposing players as victims, existing only to be destroyed.

"This four-four defense," I ask, "is it tough?"

"We can handle it. Buzz gave Jimmy Wilson a book to read on four-four." Memories of little Phil Bayer trouble me again. *They have a murderous four-four defense, so Buzz gives Jimmy Wilson a book. Michigan sends in a team, Little counters with Phil Bayer.*

Boston is cold and windy. I wander around the Ritz Hotel, stroll the Common, buy a muffler. We spend some glorious hours at the Museum of Fine Arts, but my mind and my heart are at King School. I am communing with Rubens and Rembrandt; King is battling the bad guys of the Fairchester League.

Shivering, we get back to the hotel. I call David at home. No answer. Marie is certain he is in Stamford Hospital. They broke his skull. His knee is ruined forever. And it's my fault, encouraging him to play, secretly enjoying the brutishness of it, his raw hands, charley horses, swollen jaw.

"I'm calling the coach," she says. "He's hurt."

"Calm down. I'll call the Levisons."

Andy gets on the phone. He's subdued, soft-voiced.

"Mr. Green, Andy. How did you do?"

"For God's sake, ask if David is all right!" my wife shouts.

"We lost."

"Bad?"

"Oh, fifty-five to nothing."

"I'm sorry. Gee, I'm sorry, Andy. They really put it to you, huh?"

"Ask if David is all right," Marie insists.

"Is Dave okay?"

"Yeah, sure."

"You're okay?"

"Yeah. Nobody got hurt much."

"Too bad you lost so big. I'm sorry, Andy. Hell of a way to go out."

"They intercepted six passes and ran five of them back for touchdowns. Something like that. We were never in the game."

I'm stunned. But not as stunned as I should be. The white shoes. The flags. The BEAT HACKLEY streamers. Was I right or not? Had they any right to taunt the lion? I'm glad it isn't David I'm hearing this from. He'd be all grunts, growls, annoyed dismissals of my concern.

"Big party tonight?" I ask. "The usual bash at Rut's?"

"I think so."

"Tell Dave I called. We'll see him tomorrow."

It's all over. A record of 1-6-1 isn't that bad. It could have been worse. They were almost 4-4, I keep telling myself. Like a chant, a cabalistic formula, we will keep repeating that all winter. *We*

could have been 4-4. Even 5-3. Only St. Luke's, Hackley, and first
Rye were really lost. By January, we belie, e it. But secretly, I am
settling for 1-6-1. It has a nice symmetry. We brought football
back to King.

Later I will learn that, despite Andy's assurances that no one
was badly hurt, the team absorbed a terrible physical beating.
Cameron Sillars sustained three broken ribs. Rick Hart, a reserve
lineman, suffered a concussion. Bob Fieber aggravated an injured
elbow and will need surgery. David limped off the field with the
worst of his several charley horses.

Rex Harrison sits silently through the banquet at Boston University. Did his son lose 55-0 that afternoon? Stern-faced, with
eyes downcast, he talks not at all to Dr. Gotlieb and the other officers of the university. Marie darts jealous glances at the actor,
the Mike Siganos of the English theater. He has all the moves.
(But can he *stuff*?) When he rises to thank Boston University for
honoring him with a degree and accepting his papers, he speaks
briefly, almost apologetically. He seems heavy in the jaw. There
is applause. He sits down. My fellow guests of honor are Ilka
Chase and Anya Seton. We're all polite to one another, but we
keep our distance. As the band plays airs from *My Fair Lady*, I
want to grab people and tell them about the St. Hugh's game.

Back at the Ritz, I can't sleep. I keep seeing the King team, humiliated, dragging themselves off the field. Buzz is raging. David
is crying. The season dying on a cold November day. All the glory
gone. All hopes of victory shattered. Did Fieber spin? Wilson
fumble? Levison get penalized? Dave go offside? I thank God
that it is at long last over. He need never play football again.

"Was Rex Harrison worth it?" I yawn. Outside, the lights of
Boston wink in the cold night.

"He's beautiful. But he didn't seem to talk much."

We doze. I'm glad I missed the Hackley game. Better to remember the boys frozen in action at the end of the St. Hugh's
game—laughing, dirty, savoring their small slice of the big cake.

I want it all, says Mr. Yablans. Can we not also find room for Peretz's hero Bontsha, who in Paradise asks only for a hot roll with butter?

We decide to end the season with a screening of the Hackley film—and the St. Hugh's film to take away the bitterness—at our house. Buzz comes. And Fieber, Andy, Wilson, Sillars, LeBlanc, Rut, a few others. Coach Stanley is feeling mellow, autumnal. It could have been worse. He started with nothing, ended up with a bit more than nothing, had them on the road back. Now he's got basketball to worry about. But he's confident. Not much height, but some fast kids. (They will end their season 1-16.)

"We tried a new defense," Buzz says. "A six-one to stop Hackley outside. They used a four-four, and they were a tough team defensively. God, they led St. Luke's until the last quarter. The book on Hackley was they were big and tough but couldn't move the ball."

"One of their kids told the St. Luke's headmaster to fuck himself," Levison says, with wonder in his voice.

"That was okay," Buzz says moodily. "He didn't know he was the headmaster. They talk that way to everyone."

"Two guys had the BEAT HACKLEY streamers ripped off their backs," Andy laughs. "Edge and Espo."

"Yeah," Dave says. "They kept mocking us. 'What the hell is that for? Who do you assholes think you are?' "

We look at the screen. It's the disaster I have always feared.

When we screen films, Buzz supplies a running commentary—witty, pungent, even when King is being annihilated. The boys, sipping their cans of beer, are still capable of laughing at their defeat. It is the laughter of relief.

"Two things happened on the first play from scrimmage that set the tone," Buzz explains. The film rolls. Hackley, in satanic black, looks fearsome. Small Oakland Raiders, even to the silver trim.

"What two things?" I ask.

"Fieber fumbled and Andy started swapping shots with Guzzo."

"They were offsetting penalties," Andy says. "It wouldn't have hurt except for Bobby's fumble."

Bob ducks his head. I want him to be left alone. He gained over 600 yards in five games. Had he played all season he would be a cinch for All-League. A little less spinning, less fumbling, he'd make All-State.

"It begins to disintegrate at this point," Buzz says.

A huge form looms in the King secondary, catches a dump pass, twists and turns sixty-five yards for a touchdown.

"Yeah, Guzzo," Buzz mutters. "Mori and Barrett bounced off him. They had good shots at him, but he had too much size and speed."

King gets the ball and is helpless. Sillars fumbles, Wilson falls on it. Boe is inundated by black jerseys.

"They dominated us," David says, "They blew us out."

"You were grunting?" I ask.

"You know it. They hit harder than St. Luke's."

It's not one of Mean Joe's better efforts. He overruns a punt. Hackley is downfield quickly. A back breaks loose. Dave sticks him, but he gains ten yards. A short pass, with Dave out of position in the 4-3 (linebacker is not his best spot), and they're on the ten.

It's Sillars's turn to be out of position on the next play. He makes a hard tackle, but the back falls into the end zone. On the extra-points try, no one covers the man in motion, and a short pass makes it 14-0.

"It is at this point," Coach Stanley says, "that I realized we are being beaten. They are shoving it down our throat. They are making us choke on our pride."

"We were still trying," David says defensively.

"Not hard enough."

On the kick-off, Sillars is crushed by six black jerseys. He gets up stumbling, disoriented. Hackley shows its contempt for the King offense by not even covering a slot back. Fieber manages a four-yard gain, each inch a wrenching effort. On the next play six black jerseys smother *him*.

"Terrible," Buzz muses. "We were intimidated, for the first time all year. Even St. Luke's . . ."

King holds. But it's no use. Hackley's punt rolls downfield. At the quarter it's still only 14-0. Maybe they can turn it around. Vaamonde, a ninth-grader, fourteen years old, makes a good catch. He's tall and limber, a prospect. Stanley goes to the passing game. Old riverboat gambler, he has a hunch. Maybe Sam Boe can turn the trick with those quarterback-in-motion plays. But one completion does not a successful game plan make. The next pass is short. The next is intercepted and run back fifty yards for a touchdown. With the extra points, it's 22-0.

Silence in my living room.

"Here's where I took Dave out," Buzz says moodily. "He wasn't sticking. He was down on himself."

It's over, thank the Lord. The bloody season's over. No more of this torment. David finds his beer-clotted voice. "Dammit, they killed us from the start. The game got away."

"You were crying," Stanley says.

More silence.

"It's nothing to be ashamed of," Buzz says. "You wanted to end the season in style. You people just never got it together."

Boe is smeared. He looks dazed. Fieber drops a pass. The tackling is murderous, vicious. They swarm on the ballcarrier. Arms and fists fly, yet they are never penalized.

"The refs expect this of Hackley. They get away with everything." Buzz's explanation is no help. They've swept an end for a long run and it's 30-0.

"I admitted defeat also," Buzz confesses. "Normally I stay in shirt sleeves, no matter how cold. It was freezing, and I put my jacket on. Iggy Haims saw me do it, and he said, 'Coach, you're gonna get bombed tonight.' I did."

Boe is intercepted again. A quarterback sweep. It is 36-0 at halftime.

"You took me out because I had a charley horse," David says defensively.

"Yeah, but you were down on yourself," Buzz says. "Everything we worked for was falling apart; we were getting killed."

"Boe was damn near hysterical," Andy says. "Shouting, crying. Guzzo was pushing him into the ground, laughing when he did it."

There's a moment of comic relief before the half ends. David gets behind Fieber and pushes his ass five yards forward. "It's illegal," Stanley says, "but it was one of our biggest gains of the day."

Fieber spins again before the halftime whistle. "Joe Spin," Buzz says to him. "Bobby, show us the bruises on your back from getting hit from the rear."

"It's no joke," Fieber says. "My elbow needs surgery."

Sillars, they will discover in January, suffered cracked ribs when half the Hackley team fell on him.

"What did you say at halftime?" I ask Buzz.

"What could I say? 'You guys stink. You have no pride. Go on out and make it a ball game.'"

"It wasn't just that they hit you so hard," Bob Ficber explains. "A whole crowd of them, laying into you, punching, grabbing, anything they could hide from the ref. It was what they called you."

I ask: "What did they say?"

Fieber is a proper boy, from a family of high achievers. He hesitates before answering, our tragic hero, looks to the coach for permission.

"Tell him," Buzz says.

"They'd hit you," Fieber says, "and you'd get called MF and CS and SOB. Not once. Twenty times. They kept yelling at you when you went down. They all took turns telling you what they thought."

My skin prickles. "And what could you do?"

"Nothing. If you dared to call *them* a name they'd hit you even harder and call you more names on the next tackle."

"A nice bunch of kids," Buzz says.

By now I am grateful not only that the season is over but that David need never play another game of football. Let him stick to hockey, tennis, skiing, golf. Enough of this destructive insanity.

"Jesus, look what they do to Rick Hart," Stanley says.

Hart is a junior lineman who may take David's place next season. Stanley runs the film backward and forward—frame by frame—so we can savor the horror. Hart is blocked, goes down, driven into the earth face down, as if by a giant hammer. His face, his helmet, seem to be three inches below the grass.

"Watch him roll over," Stanley says. "He didn't know where he was."

"Was it a concussion?" Rut asks.

"Yeah. His pupils were dilated. I had to break an ammonia capsule under his nose. I asked him what position he played. No answer. He sat on the bench for the rest of the game. He had X rays today. Negative, but he's woozy. One of the assistants tried to send him back in at tackle, and Rick knew enough to refuse. Said he was a guard. No point in getting killed."

Small favors again. I'm thankful David got his hardest shot on the last play of the St. Luke's game. It seems aeons ago, a thousand afternoons away. We're in some dark tunnel. I want a happier ending to this King football season. Where is it? Not on the fluttering film. It's 43-0.

"After the game I told the refs off," Stanley says. "But good."

The boast sounds thin and hollow in the night. This isn't the Buzz we know. Boe is intercepted again. We're at 49-0.

"We had a few good gains until Guzzo stuck Sillars," Andy says. "Boy, was Cam in pain."

"It still hurts," Sillars says. He spaces his words—uncertain, thoughtful.

Again, I'm trying to find literary models for the season. St. Hugh's was our *War and Peace*—noble, eternal, inspiring. What is Hackley? It's the dark night of the soul, the descent into the maelstrom. It lacks the dignity of an *Inferno*, but it is full of horror and suffering. I'm not sure what it is. I'm sorry it happened.

Fourth quarter: more misery. Dave opens a vast hole in the Hackley line, shoving two linemen away. Unfortunately, Fieber runs the wrong way. He makes a few yards. It doesn't matter. Guzzo intercepts and runs it back for a touchdown. We've reached the depths, the final disastrous count, 55-0.

"I can't believe it," Buzz muses. "We're moving. We went fifty yards, running right at them on this series."

"Until they intercepted Boe," Fieber says.

The drama's done. I'm waiting for Ishmael's coffin to be hurled up from the whirlpool. Tashtego must nail the sea bird to the bowsprit of the *Pequod*. But I need something more. Fantast that I am, failed athlete, a faker who walked pigeon-toed to fool people into thinking I had good moves, I wait for a redeeming act, something that will raise me from my Slough of Despond.

"Look at Bobby go," Stanley says. "This was it, the thing that started it."

"Started what?" I ask.

"The fight."

"Who won?"

"It was a draw, but it felt good."

On the edge of my seat, I can't wait. Something will be saved. *Some work of noble note may be done, not unbecoming men who strove like gods . . .* We may be beaten, but we can fight. Fourteen-year-olds against nineteen-year-olds. The town bullies thrashed by the hero. Shane riding into the sunset. American mythology demands it. It's *High Noon*, and Gary Cooper has to walk that dusty street.

On the screen, Fieber is off again, dragging tacklers with him. The breaks to the sidelines. He won't go down. Spinning, he loses enough speed for five black jerseys to smash into him. He's still on his feet, lunging, striding, as they fall out of bounds. Guzzo is swinging him around in wide, humiliating circles.

The film flickers, cuts to the next play.

"Where's the fight?" I ask.

The coach stops the projector. "They didn't film it. It's not part of the game. Makes the league look bad."

"Tell me about it."

Buzz jerks a thumb at David. "Mean Joe started it."

"Started—?"

David sips his beer. "Yeah. I got sick of those guys roughing up Bob. They were laying into him."

"What did you do?" I ask. In my marbled mind, I'm getting my lumps again in Brooklyn. Coming home with a torn cap, a tearful report about a stolen football.

"What did he *do?*" Buzz retorts, exultant. "He waded into Guzzo swinging."

"You land any?" I ask.

"It was all mixed up. I hit him, he hit me, and we went down."

"The benches empty," Buzz says. The coach gets up. He's enjoying it. "I got there first and grabbed Guzzo by the throat. I said to him, 'Cut it out, or I'll tear your face off.' Levison was in the middle of the pile. Everyone else was on top."

"And me and Guzzo on the bottom," Dave says. He says it offhandedly. He has not the vaguest idea what he is doing for me.

"The refs stopped it?" I ask.

"Yeah," Buzz says. "They peeled guys off. I never heard so many 'MF's' in my life. That must be the name of a course they teach at Hackley."

Rag LeBlanc laughs. "I was holding Mean Joe back. He wanted to get at Guzzo again."

"I was glad you were," David says.

"You should have been thrown out," Buzz says. "You swung first." *Swung first!* And how do you like it now, gentlemen?

"Guzzo was tossed out. He and one other Hackley guy. For punching Bobby." David reveals this with no pride, no sense of achievement. He wanted the game. The fight was the result of frustration, anger that could not be stemmed.

"It was beautiful," Andy Levison says. "Just getting a few swings at those guys in the pile. I think we fought them even in the fight, or maybe had an edge. Two of their guys out, Dave still in."

"Boe had his helmet ripped off," Sillars says sadly. He sits stiffly, aching, unaware of his broken ribs. I grieve for Rick Hart, dazed and misty-eyed.

The film resumes. I bask in the glow of the battle royal I never saw. I have my happy ending. I don't care about the score. We fought back. We didn't take the insult like cowards. Mean Joe swung first.

On the screen, it's the old King story. They're inside the Hackley fifteen-yard line. The white-shirted team runs repeatedly inside the fifteen-yard line, fails to score. As the film rolls inexorably to its end, as Dave's football career marches into history, I hear French horns. Something poignant, rich, all passion spent—like the haunting notes in the first scene of *Der Rosenkavalier.*

"Guzzo and I shook hands at the end," David says.

Better yet. Better and better. He is accepted into the brotherhood of violence.

"What did he say?" I ask him. Sunset and evening star. The season is over. And so is a compartment of our lives.

"Oh, good game, all that crap. He said he couldn't believe I got him thrown out."

Buzz shuts off the projector, I put on the room lamps. I have my literary parallel. Hackley was a private-eye yarn—Hammett or Chandler. The hero drubbed, beaten, cheated, humiliated, but rising again, coming back, winning a small victory, asserting his superiority before the tale of bloody vengeance ends. Sam Spade. The Continental Op. Marlowe.

"I laid it on the line with their coach when the game was over," Buzz says. "He's my friend, but what the hell."

He threads up St. Hugh's; a final look at glory. A decent man, a hardworking man, surely a man who knows football, Buzz deserves a happier future. If I had it in my power, I'd start recruiting for him—swift blacks and giant Poles and mean Italians, the street kids of Bridgeport and Norwalk. He'll need them.

"Oh, before we run this," Buzz says, "everybody get a load of these season statistics for all eight games." He distributes mimeographed sheets.

"Wow," David says. "We ran up a hundred and twenty-eight first downs to our opponents seventy-two."

"Yards rushing," Fieber adds, "King 1,574; opponents 1,358. If you leave out St. Luke's and Hackley, we outran everybody."

No one deserves Bobby's tribute more than Bobby. He was the offense. He ran without stopping for the five games he played.

"Only problem was," Buzz says, "we fumbled forty times to our opponents' twenty-six. That's an average of five fumbles a game for us, and most of them inside the twenty-yard line. No way to play winning football."

"I can't believe these stats," David says softly. "We should have been four-four."

"Even five-three," Andy says. He lights a cigarette.

"Put out that butt, you fool," Buzz reprimands him. "Your body belongs to me."

"Not any more, coach."

11

In the winter there's a sports banquet. We all show up, the fathers looking fat and embarrassed, the boys appearing somewhat smaller than we remember them during the football season. Only John Rutledge seems as huge as ever. David, dieting, getting his weight down for hockey, looks shrunken.

David wins the award for best defensive player, also the sportsmanship award, which is given for leadership and manliness. The latter, I gather, is a tribute to his battle with Guzzo. He also makes the All-Fairchester League first team, as an offensive guard. It isn't his best position, but I'll settle for it. Where he really excelled, Buzz tells me, was at nose guard, down in the muck, in the center of the line, clawing, scuttling crablike, clutching at legs and knees. But a nose guard is a freak of sorts. All-star defensive teams are usually picked with a four-man front, three linebackers, and a four-man defensive secondary. There's no room for the odd man up front, the bloody, dirty middle man, head to head with the center.

It's cold and starry as we walk into the Connecticut night. David is lugging his trophies. *All-Fairchester League.* He's up there with Siganos and Smith and Robinson, all his ancient enemies. A long season, but they weren't disgraced. They never quit. He certainly didn't. You don't stick your helmet into Steve Smith with the clock running out if you're a quitter.

185

"Did I ever tell you how I won an intramural softball medal at Columbia in my senior year?" I ask him, as we drive home.

"Softball? Since when were you a softball player?"

We live out our lives trying to prove to our sons that we are real men, heroes, successes. Nothing less is demanded of us. "I could always hit. And catch flies. The team was in the independent league. There were two leagues, the independents and the fraternities. The fraternities had all the jocks. Our league was mostly commuters, oddballs. Don Mankiewicz was our manager. He named the team the Royal Elite Cuban Giants."

"What kind of name is that?"

It's hard to explain. When David was born, Jackie Robinson had already crossed the color line. He cheered for Mays and Aaron and Ernie Banks. "It's a combination of all the names that black teams used in the 'thirties and 'forties."

He laughs. "Were there any blacks on your team?"

"No. It was Mank's idea of a joke. I played center field, sometimes first base. I hit eight singles in a row in two games. Our star pitcher was a big guy named Bill Hochman. He's a professor of history in Colorado now. I met him at the Democratic convention in Chicago in 1968."

Silence and darkness in Fairfield County. US 1 flickers with gin mills, filling stations, used-car dealers. The story of my softball triumph is left unfinished. Didn't we get beaten by the fraternity champions, 5-4? And wasn't I called out on strikes with the tying run on base? Or was that a different year? Somewhere I have the softball medal—a light blue C with a roaring lion enclosed. My name engraved on the back. It isn't quite David's armload of trophies, but it proves we're related. At least, I deceive myself, all that muscle and poise didn't come from his grandfathers, those hard, fearless men.

Bitonto Cathedral is finished. On a snowy day, David ports it to school for the judgment of Mrs. Eastman, the art history teacher. It's colorful and reasonably accurate, but we've faked the apse. I can't seem to find a floor plan for Norman Romanesque.

The windows are good, and the Magic Markers did a fair job. A few days later, David gets it back with a B-minus. "Mrs. Eastman says the apse is all wrong," he tells me. "We did it in one piece and it's supposed to have three sections."

"Three?"

"Yeah. A big semicircle in the middle, and two smaller ones."

She's right. I check the book again, and I've missed a sentence. "A triapsidal east end . . ." I'm angry with myself. If I can't help the boy win football games, at least I should be able to assist him with his cathedrals. Still, a B-minus isn't quite as bad as an offside penalty inside the ten-yard line.

The cathedral comes home, rests on the sagging Ping-Pong table, and I find myself, over the dark winter, staring at it. The colors fade, the walls droop, and the faked apse comes loose. But I haven't the heart to throw it out. It's the last cooperative effort involving Marie, myself, and one of the children. From now on, all three of our issue will be enlarging the distances between us. It won't be a case of generation gap. They'll simply have less time for us, less need for us. It's why I have clung to this pitiful football season so desperately. One hundred yards of green grass, striped white, thumped and gouged by my son and his teammates and their enemies (confound their knavish tricks!) are hardly Elysian fields. But they've given me a last gulp of parental air, a brief period of communion with my son. It won't last. It can't.

But the glory is not ended. I'm at my typewriter on a rainy afternoon. Marie is at school. The house is silent, the phone off the hook, Caesar snoozing at my feet. The writing is going badly. It's been three months since I came back from Manila, frustrated, lighter by $2,000. It's been difficult cranking up again, especially with all the sleep I've been losing over 4-3 zones, 6-2 tackle wides, and 5-3 gap thunders.

"Dad, how come we don't get the *Daily News?*" David asks.

He's standing in the door of my study—dark, broad-shouldered, looking as if he is about to throw a block or ram his helmet into a runner's midriff.

"Mother and I prefer the *Times*."

"Andy Levison says I made the *Daily News* all-star team."

"What?"

"Yeah. It says King School, Dave Green. It's the Fairfield County All-Stars. But it was last Sunday, and no one has a copy."

As if propelled by an ejector, I spring from my swivel chair. A fluttery migraine is gone. The strange pains in my knees and ankles vanish. "Let's go," I say. "The Stamford Library will have it on file."

They do. I make a Xerox copy. We have small time for the first and second teams, loaded with talent from the big local high schools. Under Honorable Mention we find it. The listings are alphabetical. "KING SCHOOL: DAVE GREEN."

"Hmmm. Sounds black. A black wide receiver."

David laughs. "Hey," he says. "Siganos got jobbed. He only made Honorable Mention also."

Siganos is indeed snubbed. Because he played for a small prep school, he is ignored on the first and second teams. (Whitcomb, I learn, is furious. And he has a right to be. Siganos can run rings around all the first- and second-team backs.)

No one else from King, St. Luke's, Hamden Hall, or Brunswick —the Fairfield County teams in the Fairchester League—makes the *News* squad. It's another one of those heady plateaus. An apotheosis for my son. It won't end my migraines, but it will be worth a thousand conversations. My Americanism need never be doubted. For the remaining years of my life, I can wander among the Gentiles, making casual reference to the boy who made the *Daily News All-Star Fairfield County Team.* At long last, I am a member of that brotherhood of jockery that ranges from Mr. O'Dowd with his American flag to Mailer to the ghosts of Hemingway and Steinbeck.

The Xerox copies will go into the folder we've been keeping on the King School football season. We even make a copy of the lead story ("ALL-STARS HAVE SAVVY TO SPARE") so we will know in years to come the good company Dave was in.

At home, displaying the news items to Marie—who is under-whelmed, more concerned with David's sinking College Board scores—I announce that I am going to call Mailer.

"Why?" she asks. She adores Mailer.

"Oh, just in general. 'Hello, Norman, baby?' I will say. 'Sorry, Norm baby, but my kid got there first. *Daily News* team, you see. All those construction workers and cops and longshoremen. Get it? The kid did it on his own. It must have been those sixteen un-assisted tackles against Hamden Hall.' "

But I never call. It's enough to drop it casually into conversations. At a dinner party in Greenwich, surrounded by people who are weeping for Nixon, recalling the good old days when John Mitchell rounded up long-haired traitors and shoved them into jails, I explode. "You can all start baking cakes," I bellow at the women. "You can hide files in them and mail them to Mr. Mitchell when he goes to jail!" I don't fear them any longer.

Under counterattack, forced to defend Teddy Kennedy (I ab-stain), I find myself switching the table talk to football and David. I am no longer the Enemy of the People. It dawns on me —I'm in a charitable mood, surrounded by these lacquered heads and Scotch-flushed faces—why poor Nixon spent so much time among jocks, why he found it obligatory to phone assurances to Lenny Dawson but had no words for the bereaved parents of the students killed at Kent State. *He's an outsider too.* To connect he courted men of violence, those who *stick.* Is it possible we're a na-tion of outsiders, a rootless folk, trying to reassure ourselves of lost honor, vanished glory, with rough games and triumphs? I hope not.

So it's all over. Fixed, framed, compartmentalized in my mind's eye, those brightly colored afternoons at King School. Like F. Scott Fitzgerald's years at Princeton, they have for me—and I hope for David—a limited perfection, a circumscribed excellence that nothing can ever equal.

Fitzgerald poignantly recalled a vanished Princeton halfback, his head bandaged in the era when helmets were optional, kicking from behind his own goal line in the cold dusk of a November day. My memories are more modest, but enough for me. David chasing the giant, falling on the mad bouncing football. ("I prayed it wouldn't go out of bounds," he confessed.) Or barreling toward the sidelines in front of Bobby Fieber, hurling his hard body at a defensive back. Or, for God's sake, weeping on the sidelines as Hackley dismembered the team, and then returning to lead the free-for-all. The frustrations of middle age, the headaches, the bad reviews, the political heroes defeated, assorted agonies and setbacks—all of these will be a little easier to take. Don't ask me why. Don't force me to admit that I'm behaving childishly, too much involved in a game, and not even as a participant. Oh, but it's done something for me. I don't necessarily believe in the sign in Buzz's office that proclaims "SUCCESS IS THE RESULT OF HARD WORK AND HONEST EFFORT." Nor am I sold on President Bear Bryant. But I've changed, and a seventeen-year-old was largely responsible.

O'Neill knew the marrow-deep truth of American life: We desperately need our illusions, myths and fables to help us get from one day to the next. The drunks in Harry Hope's saloon aren't much different from most of us. We all cultivate our gardens, and some are full of exotic growths, tropical blossoms and trailing vines that no one except the gardener ever sees or sniffs. Full of dreams and hopes, troubled by muffed chances and lost loves, we savor the fragrance, marvel at the florid colors.

No longer do I care that King lost six games, or should have won three or four of them, or fumbled too much. And maybe Dave wasn't quite the star I imagined him to be. Sometimes he missed a tackle or got blown out. But he did his best, and he did not quit, and he was not afraid, and he was a leader. He earned a respect that eluded me all my boyhood, and what more can I ask?

The years will enlarge the canvas and intensify the colors. In my seventies, I'll recall to a hard-of-hearing audience around a Fort Lauderdale shuffleboard court that my son was All-State, weighed 210, captained an undefeated team. Like Hickey, I'll nourish my "lying pipedreams," and why not? The myths are relatively harmless and they help us get over those rougher moments of life, which, as Dr. Johnson knew, contained more that was to be endured than enjoyed.

Over the summer, faced with another losing season, Buzz recruits a star running back from one of the local high schools. He has the terrifying name of Mickey Koczeniak. He's 6′ 3″, 220 pounds, and he needs no blockers, dragging tacklers with him five, ten, fifteen yards. Another shrewd ploy by the Buzzer: He moves Ralph Esposito, the rugged tight end, to quarterback. Jimmy Wilson, light and fast, becomes a wide receiver. Almost at once, Buzz creates an offense—Koczeniak running, Espo throwing. A few big seniors, less shy than those of last year's batch who refused to be enticed by David's appeals, come out for the team. The result is a 5-5 season, with wins over Rye, Deaf, Trinity, Fieldston, and of course, poor St. Hugh's. Rye is so badly battered by Koczeniak that it gives up the rest of its season.

And what of last year's heroes, the "hapless" few who brought the game back to King? I see them on occasional weekends. Andy, Bobby, Rut, and Dave are there for the St. Hugh's game. Homecoming again. Buzz knows when he has a good thing. It's a romp, 29-0. On the sidelines, Dave and the others seem strangely ambivalent. They're glad King is winning games again, but why couldn't *they* have won a few more? I'm on the edge of explaining that life can't be lived in terms of might-have-beens, but I suspect they're ahead of me.

Last summer, Murray Levison, with whom I prowled the sidelines, was killed in an automobile accident. I worry about Andy and his sisters. Their mother died a few years ago. Relatives are looking after them. But Andy seems calm, mature. Maybe football helped. He's at Alfred University now. Like the rest of the old guard, he's eschewing college football. Dave at Ithaca, Bobby at Vermont, Rut at Tufts have decided they've thrown their last blocks.

The big news is that Mike Siganos is starting at Kentucky, a football power. They've made a safety man out of him, and already he's intercepted four passes, run one back for a touchdown. I sense that some of the glory reaches them. After all, they waved at Siganos all afternoon a year ago.

I leave at halftime. It's not the same. Koczeniak is very good. He will win the Fairchester League scoring title and go on to a great college career. But I miss Fieber spinning and bouncing, Dave plunging into the opponents' backfield.

In the evening I find myself foolishly shooting fouls again, trying to break the Sawmill Road record. I fail. David chooses not to join me. There's talk of a hockey game somewhere. He leaves me alone on the sloping driveway, dreaming that I'm Walt Frazier or Jerry West. The life in David is like Thoreau's rising river, flooding my parched uplands and drowning the muskrats of gloom that lurk in my nature.

I sink a last foul shot and move slowly into the house. *Exits followed by a retriever.* The house seems to get emptier and emptier, deprived of children, beer cans, hockey equipment, rock music, ski poles. I wasn't cheering too loudly at the game this afternoon. Maturity or old age? Sandburg said the past is a bucket of ashes. I'm not too sure. For me there's a green field on a clear autumn day, and the flash of a shiny white football helmet and a maroon 51.